W9-ARV-136

In Appreciation

We have been fortunate, over more than 60 years, to have worked for and with five generations of the Kessinger family as a reporter, editor and executive of the Rome *Sentinel*.

When we joined the *Sentinel* news staff, in 1926, Augustus C. Kessinger, who purchased the weekly *Sentinel* in 1864, was at his desk every day. He was succeeded by his son, Albert R. Kessinger, and the family line has been continued by Bradley C. and Margaret Kessinger Barnard, George and Shirley Barnard Waters, and Stephen B. and Wendy Williams Waters.

George and Shirley Waters suggested and made possible this book. We appreciate their encouragement and support.

Excerpts from our 18-year-old weekly column are reprinted with the permission of the Rome Sentinel Company.

FRITZ S. UPDIKE's

POTATO HILL AND OTHER RECOLLECTIONS

Published by
North Country Books, Inc.
18 Irving Place
Utica, New York 13501-5618

Fritz S. Updike's
Potato Hill
and
Other Recollections

Copyright © 1988
by Fritz S. Updike

All Rights Reserved
No part of this book may be reproduced
in any manner without written
permission of the publisher.

ISBN 0-932052-71-1

Library of Congress Cataloging-in-Publication Data
Updike, Fritz. 1905-
    Fritz Updike's Potato Hill and other recollections.
        1. Updike, Fritz. 1905-   . 2. Rome Region (N.Y.)—
Biography. 3. Rome Region (N.Y.)—Social life and customs.
I. Title.   II. Title: Potato Hill and other recollections.
F129.R82U638   1988   974.7'62   88-31478
ISBN 0-932052-71-1

Published by
North Country Books, Inc.
Publisher—Distributor
18 Irving Place
Utica, New York 13501-5618

Foreword

If all the verbal requests, letters and notes wishing Fritz would assemble a collection of his weekly columns in book form were totaled it would stretch the capacity of most modern day calculators.

Long the favorite of the majority of Friday *Sentinel* readers the column has graced the pages of the newspaper for more years than any other. Editorial pages are not the best read according to surveys yet his contribution has made that page on that day one of the most eagerly awaited.

Why? Probably there is not a cut and dried answer but we can speculate. There is a dual value in his writings. Memories are refreshed for the older audience . . . and the human race dotes on fond memories growing richer over the years. In the second place the past ten years have seen an explosion of interest on the part of the younger generation in their family tree and in the way their forbears lived. Fritz's column appeals to both groups.

Shirley and I, as fourth generation caretakers of the *Sentinel*, sensitive to our heritage and secure in the knowledge that our Friday writer was one of the most respected journalists in a demanding trade, decided to do something about the requests. Potato Hill should come alive between the covers of a book.

Fritz had always said he'd get around to putting it all together some day but, being human, procrastinated. Now he had no excuse and a real incentive. Fine newsman that he is, the challenge could not be turned down.

It was not easy. What do you save, what should you keep? What must go by the board? Writing that looked so good at the time didn't ring as true as it might today. And when you are pounding it all out on a typewriter so old fresh ribbons had to be wound upon old reels and keys so used they required not just a touch but a push, it was an effort and a chore. In our business, as with any writer, working out and rewriting an initial story is where it's at. None of us like to copy by rote.

Day after day sitting within the protective and familiar walls of his office, Fritz hacked away striving to meet the demands and deadlines set by his publisher. There can be little question but that the discipline of years in the trade (beginning on December 15, 1926, his first day with this paper) held him up and helped him through.

Husband, father, grandfather, great-grandfather, civic servant and leader, a man with a hearty laugh, convivial by nature, adept at the art of dig and poker, noted locally and nationally as an historian, the list of his achievements and gifts to the human race could fill pages. Yet we think of him, and are sure he does of himself, as a consumate journalist in the true sense of the word. This cannot be said of many. The thread of his life and that of the *Sentinel* and its families have been intimately interwoven and we are all the richer for it.

"Long live Potato Hill," to quote our mutual friend, Brick Hasfield!

—George B. Waters

Introduction

Readers of our newspaper column, from which this book is taken, have had problems distinguishing between our early childhood on Potato Hill with our maternal grandparents and teenage years with our Mother and Father on their farm atop the next higher ridge.

That difficulty may persist here. When we were less than five years old, we lived with Grandpa and Grandma most of each year and, thereafter, each summer until we were 13. In teenage days, when our parents were seeking a living on their farm, we helped until we went for two years to preparatory school and one year at college. (Our folks hardly had the money, but Mother insisted.)

Grandpa and Grandma were married when he returned from cavalry duty in the Civil War. He was a short, stocky man, of around 190 pounds, fun to be with. She was a little woman of about 90 pounds, daughter of a substantial family which, Mother said, was related to Commodore Oliver Hazard Perry of War of 1812 fame. Grandma dressed in black, her only splash of color her ever-present gingham apron. Grandpa was an orphan, adopted by a German family.

The farm house we knew so well, not stately but spacious and comfortable, burned after Grandma had moved off the farm when Grandpa died. She survived him by 18 years. Their house and barns have disappeared. There is no sign of past habitation aside from a cellar hole filled with brush, and an old well hole off to one side. The wonderful view in all directions, particularly over the southern end of Seneca Lake, is still there.

This is a collection of pieces, long and short, of recollections of life on Potato Hill, of days with our family up the hill a piece; of 50 years and 15 active days with the Rome *Sentinel*, not counting off-and-on journalism activity during 11 years of retirement.

It will seem that we have neglected our paternal grandparents.

We did not have the opportunity to be with them, except for occasional brief visits. They lived a ways off, in those days of horse and buggy, but were always kind to us. That Grandmother baked wonderful cookies; Grandfather told gripping stories and supplied us with old dime novels—on the sly. A carpenter, he was the eighth generation of a Holland Dutchman who came to New Amsterdam before 1653. A cemetery and a country road near his place bear the family name.

Our Potato Hill grandparents, Samuel R. (1841-1917) and Sarah Canfield Sherrer (1850-1935) in what are believed to be their wedding photos.

Our paternal grandparents, Daniel (1845-1924) and Delphine Cole Updike as a young girl (1848-1925).

George and Stella Updike, Mom and Dad, with the author.

PART I

On Grandpa's Farm

On Grandpa's Farm

THE PLACE OF DREAMS

There were poignant tales of the past in the remains of an old orchard on the thin-soil, rocky hill high above the lake. Neglected, ancient fruit trees can tell a meaningful story for those who understand.

When the young veteran who sired our mother returned from the Civil War, he took a young girl of sturdy farm stock as his bride. They built their modest home on Potato Hill, adding to the original structure as the family grew.

Among the first requirements was the planting of an orchard, between the house and the barn, 70 yards or so of open land, traversed by a path. One day in some unrecorded spring, apple trees arrived at the railroad freight house in the village. The two probably dreamed over the catalogue for hours, choosing among the Baldwins, Northern Spies, Pippins, Palm Sweets and others of that time.

The orchard, a stonewall on one side, the dirt road on another, the house and the barn at each end, was well tended as the years passed. Children found mates and left to establish their homes. The apple trees, by then augmented with plum, peach, pear and cherry trees, continued to produce but not with the care of younger years.

Then the man and his helpmate went on ahead; the place was sold. Finally abandoned, the barns and the sheds collapsed and the house burned.

3

But the fruit trees remained, more gaunt each year among high weeds and tall grasses. Even so, in the heart of the winter the old orchard had a purpose. Deer came to paw the snow to uncover fallen, wizened fruit; partridges flew among the misshapened trees.

In the spring, a few pink and white blossoms would appear as the few surviving trees, more than 100 years old, sought to obey the summons of Nature.

Then, one day, the present owner of the land cleared off the homesite, eliminating the last traces of the orchard, along with the well and the cellar hole. He did not realize the significant part of personal history that old farm site occupied with one who no longer returns to turn on the dreams of recollections.

Yet, everyone should have time in this unpredictable world for day dreams. We write, for our own enjoyment, about a hilly farm, searching in memory for small happenings of a long-ago childhood, events that meant little then, much now.

We may not remember what happened last week, but events of seven and eight decades ago are as of yesterday. Details may be hazy, but our young life on Potato Hill with an understanding grandmother and an easy-going, lovable grandfather is etched in time.

Most of our grandchildren have accompanied us to the site of that farm, on the third eastern ridge high above the southern end of Seneca Lake. All they saw was a vacant cellar hole, an unprotected well and a pile of brush marking the old cellar. Someone now plants corn on what was once the small, but productive orchard between the house and barns. None of the old rail fences remain.

Our visiting kin are impressed more with the as-far-as-one-can-see view, over the lake and down the southern valley, than they are with the memories of their grandfather. They can drive away from that spot to explore those far-off vistas at will; they do not realize that, as a young boy, we could only look in vain, wondering if we would ever go into that world over the horizon, the places we had heard grown folks talk about.

It is best, for us, to go there alone. To simply stand in solitude by the site of Grandma's lilac bushes that marked the corner of the woodshed. To look across the now open land and see Grandpa's fields and the land to the woodlot, where he taught us to enjoy nature.

It is a perfect spot for day dreaming, of happy times without adult responsibilities, of the simple fun of being with a grand old man, of being watched over and well nourished by a strict but loving grandmother.

Day dreams . . . but not for long. We hasten away, moist eyed, fearing, perhaps, that we might be forced to remain forever on the hill where once we wondered if we would ever go to the other side of the lake.

Brick Hasfield says it often takes a week or more to prepare for an impromptu speech.

CLEARING THE LAND

As we travel about the countryside, nearly all of us picture the open vista as the way it has been for thousands of years. Only a few consider that there was a time when most of the land had to be cleared of trees, brush and rocks, when our forefathers faced tremendous problems in creating tillable acres.

Farming in the early days of this country meant first clearing land for pastures and crops, without the convenience of modern power equipment. It is difficult to imagine the tremendous task of cutting trees, hand sawing trunks for lumber or hauling trunks and branches into piles for burning. And the stumps! Today's museums have depictions of the devices of those days for exerting power to tear and/or pry long-rooted stumps from the ground.

Our Grandfather cleared his farm on Potato Hill when he came home from the war, married the girl who was to be his life companion, purchased a sizeable tract of timber land and began to remove the trees.

First they cleared a plot at the top of the ridge and built a small house while living first in a crude hut and then in the cellar. Lumber was produced on site and cellar walls were local cobblestones bound together with mud. Next came his first barn, both structures being enlarged in years to come.

After these were up, Grandpa gave full attention to clearing fields on level parts of the hillside farm, particularly the soil-rich tract behind the barn. He knew how to attach chains to stumps and what roots to chop so that the big team could yank out the stumps and drag them to a pile to burn or for use as a root fence.

He did not have a mechanical stump puller, a tripod affair with a big worm gear, or a stone carrier, a wheeled device from which chains were placed around big stones for lifting and transportation to the big piles that eventually dotted his holdings.

We look at the well-tended farms as we travel rural territories and try to total in our minds the great amount of labor expended to clear the land, a precious part of the history of this country.

★   ★   ★

BREAKFAST!

When Mother or Grandma announced "breakfast!" everyone came to the table together, fully dressed, face washed and hair combed. Everyone, that is, but Grandpa. He came from the barn, with his "chores done" look. We are not so sure these days when, if two people eat the morning meal together, it must be Sunday.

Breakfast then was a real meal, produced by women who got up early, built the wood fire in the kitchen range and started everything "from scratch," but not pancake and biscuit dough which were built around a "starter," kept handy from day to day, week to week, month to month.

If there was cereal, it usually was oatmeal, the kind that cooked for an hour. Or cornmeal mush which we knew in those days as hasty pudding. Why "hasty" we do not know; it had to be cooked forever. Perhaps that was why it was prepared the day before and served the next morning fried in bacon grease.

After the cereal came fried eggs, with bacon or sausage, or slices of ham, all the meat produced on the farm and seasoned in the family smokehouse. And always thick slices of homemade bread or biscuits, the bread cut with a big, sharp knife. If you wanted it toasted, you held it on a large fork over the open fire in the range.

Pancakes did not come in a box or frozen from a supermarket. Anyone who ate one at a time would be looked upon as a stranger. Three or four were piled on each other, properly lubricated one to the other, and drowned in syrup—if not maple, corn syrup, a store product.

Grownups had coffee, a youngster hot chocolate. No one hurried and a child had to sit at table until the man of the house was finished. There were no coffee breaks in mid-morning. None was required.

★ ★ ★

SALT PORK AND GRAVY

Morning meals on Potato Hill endowed us with a lasting desire for substantial food to last the day. Toast and coffee do not qualify.

Grandma's other meals were much like those of any housewife in that wind-swept territory. She had a stock pot on the back of the range. Soup was for the asking at any meal. She baked bread, muffins, biscuits, pies, cakes and cookies. And old-fashioned fried cakes.

Beans, and the meats of the farm—pork, chicken, beef—were staples. Beans were special for Saturday or Sunday night, week after week, laced with fat salt pork and protected from the elements by a thick layer of brown sugar, crusted with maple syrup.

There were no native fish on that hill, but Grandma served it often—salt cod bought in large white slabs and nailed to a beam in the cellar. Cod cakes, cod gravy, boiled cod with boiled potatoes and bread. A treat was oysters, a once-in-a-while special, in a stew or buried in crackers and baked. A quarter a quart in those days.

And, of course, potatoes in all forms, always at breakfast; chicken for Sunday, salt pork gravy often.

Grandma never said, as did our Mother, when we were in a state of emergency: "Get a slice of bread and butter." Grandma never had to discuss such needs. We knew where the fried cakes were heaped, in a big wooden dish, and that the cookie jar was not empty.

The only basic command at Grandma's table was: "Drink your milk!" She had firm ideas about putting pounds on a skinny little fellow.

Her farm-wife life was not easy. She did not slant our existence with her along easy paths. We shared with the rest of the family and we were never deprived.

Grandma was a good cook, but she never baby-sat with us. We knew—and Grandpa knew—how far we could go with her when it came to nutrition.

★   ★   ★

ECONOMICS ON THE HILL

Economics of childhood days, 1909-1911, about which I knew nothing at all, but are now proved by old statistics in Grandma's account books:

Eggs 12 cents a dozen, butter 18 cents a pound, salt 100 pounds for 20 cents, sugar $5.80 for 100 pounds, toilet soap three bars 12 cents, coffee 15 cents a pound unground, baking beans 10 cents a can, oranges and lemons 15 cents a dozen.

She sold her eggs at the village store for 8 to 10 cents a dozen, canned her own vegetables and meats and depended on the store for such things as sugar, salt, coffee and occasionally non-local fruits.

Grandma's figures show that when the dry bean and potato crops were good, financial aspects were bright with eggs, butter, poultry, excess hay and grain perhaps bringing in as much as $400 a year. Not bad in days when there were no sales or income taxes, when local taxes, county and school, might total $40, a part of which might be "worked off" by maintaining the road past the family farm.

★   ★   ★

GRANDPA SMELLED SNOW

Grandpa said he could smell snow in the air. We never doubted him; he was long in tune with Nature.

Those of us advanced in years may not relish the advent of winter (the Lady of Our House marks its coming by the state of our disposition), but most of us remember the first snows of childhood.

When we changed from heavy shoes to felts and overs on Potato Hill, we sought pictures in the new snow. It was fun to wander in an inch or more of the stuff in the orchard, scanning tracks of birds and animals, wondering if a big print was left by a bobcat and if the big bird hunting for fallen apples had been a wild turkey. Probably it was a barn cat or a crow, but we were young and we believed.

If the first snow was deep enough, we made forts—long lines of facing snow breastworks amid the fruit trees with mounted corn-cob "cannon" to be dislodged by barrages of snowballs, a certain quota of "shots" to each side to determine the outcome of the "battle."

Or we could take our homemade sled and try sliding down the hill back of the house, an unsuccessful effort after a light snowfall, but a promise of fun to come when a good depth settled down.

The first snow! We wish we had as much enthusiasm for it now as we did when we were five and alone on a hillside farm, where anything contributing to lonely play was enjoyable.

THOSE OLD CHURNS

A friend, totally unacquainted with life on an older-day farm, reported seeing a mysterious device on television. She described it as something into which cream was poured and after a series of movements butter resulted. She had never before seen a churn.

There is no mystery about butter making for those who walked directly home from school in order to "get the cows" from the pasture in time for the evening milking. Separating cream from milk and churning it into butter, with delicious buttermilk a by-product, was routine on farms in the youthful days of current seniors.

Grandma, lacking a separator, produced cream by putting milk into large, flat pans in which, encouraged by the coolness of the cellar, the cream "would rise to the top" to be skimmed off, leaving skim milk for the pigs. No paying premium prices for denuded milk for dietary purposes. We have no memory of anyone on Potato Hill cutting down on food to lose weight.

Grandma had two styles of churns. One was a small barrel which revolved by the turning of a handle, the milk "plunking" from end to end with a hearty slosh. The other was an upright affair, the necessary disturbance of the milk being produced by means of a dasher—a slatted round piece of wood attached to a handle which came up through the top of the churn.

Energy for either device was provided by a small boy, the task not being difficult although sometimes lengthy. Nothing in this is new to those who recall backroad farms. And those who never operated a churn will not be interested, probably thinking of something more modern like classic automobiles. We are not greatly attached to such. Who wants to get excited over antiques which are younger than they are?

Brick Hasfield says that before credit cards we knew for sure when we were broke.

WINTER SOUNDS ON A LONELY HILL

The dry squeak of cutter and bobsled runners on hard-packed snow; the whinnying of horses as they greeted anyone coming with feed on a cold morning.

Sleighbells in the distance; Grandpa in the shed cutting firewood; Grandma priming the suction pump in a corner of the kitchen; eggs frying on the stove.

The never-to-be forgotten two long and two short whistles of the locomotive approaching the crossing at the bottom of the hill, a lonesome, penetrating sound of the outside world.

The hungry mooing of the cows waiting to be fed; milk hitting the side of a tin pail; the dog barking in the moonlight; bacon snapping in an iron skillet; the howl of animals in the woods (Grandpa tried to make us "face up to life" by insisting it was the wail of a man-attacking wolf).

The early boasting of the rooster as he surveyed his harem; the clucking of Grandma's satisfied hens; the clank of end chains on harness traces; the protests of ungreased wheels on farm wagons.

Grandpa stomping his boots on the porch as he came in from the barn; the Edison phonograph playing "Just Before the Battle, Mother," "Tenting Tonight on the Old Campground," and "The Preacher and the Bear." The sounds of the parlor organ as Mother played "I'm Tying the Leaves So They Won't Come Down," "Rock of Ages" and "Abide With Me."

The shout of a neighbor as he drove by; wind music in the eaves; the sound of a broom handle banging on the ceiling beneath our bedroom, summoning a young boy to another day.

★ ★ ★

OLD ENOUGH, BIG ENOUGH

Grandpa believed, and so did Grandma, that when a grandson was old enough he was big enough. That's why, when between 6 and 7, we were given the job of "fixin'" potato crates.

Nowadays these are sought after for use other than carting potatoes from field to cellar to market. Then every farmer had a sufficient supply, mostly homemade, for use over and over, year after year. They were often damaged and had to be surveyed and repaired during winter months.

Fixing potato crates was not difficult work, Grandpa providing new slats for use where needed and plenty of nails to reinforce those hanging loose.

For a long time we hadn't thought about these 18x12x14 utilitarian receptacles, so sized for two purposes, to hold potatoes and to fit inside each other for empty storage. That is until our son's wife, proudly showed us "this lovely box" she had purchased for use in her daughter's abode at college.

It was a new potato crate, solid in construction, able to hold a 220-pound adult, if the sitter sat still. And, she said, it was a bargain at a craft show—only $5.50.

Grandpa made them and sold them for a quarter.

Brick Hasfield says a small town is a place where everyone knows whose check is good and whose husband isn't.

DR. GRANDMA'S REMEDIES

We keep hearing about new remedies for curing the common cold. One found out early in life that it was best not to sniffle or sneeze around Grandma. She never got around to patenting her anti-cold treatments, being too busy, we guess, keeping her family healthy in a drafty, winter-bound farmhouse.

The first installation of her primary treatment was simple. She filled a tin cup almost full with boiling water and added a table-spoon portion of the camphor salve the Watkins medicine man sold from house-to-house.

The head of the ailing child was forcibly placed over rising fumes and a heavy towel laid over patient and scented mist. Count to 20, breathe deep, she would command until the young boy came out from under, eyes running, nose canals clear.

Should sniffles persist and the young patient appear to lack the customary bounce, it was time for an onion poultice. There is little new about this often miraculous therapy; many grown men and women have memories of skin-searing chest applications.

Grandma mashed a generous batch of onions into a juicy mess, fried it to the point where it could not be held in hand, placed it between two layers of flannel and slapped the smelly, hot onion-cloth sandwich onto the bare chest, strapping it in place, as the patient cried he was "on fire," by winding strips of old sheets around the quivering body.

Not only did one's skin turn "redder than a spanked baby's

behind," as Grandpa described it, but the camphor cleaned nasal passages which retained the onion odor like that of a time-release rub-on salve.

Grandma also had an elixir to perk one up as Spring neared. She stirred powdered sulphur into sticky, dark molasses, producing one of the most evil potions of our childhood. A tablespoon would thin the blood, she insisted. This horrible mixture hastened loud declarations of perfect health.

She also had an iron tonic produced by boiling rusty nails with cherry bark, red alder bark, sassafras and pine buds. She stored it in a covered crock and Grandpa took it gladly—it was tuned with whiskey.

Speaking of modern colds, Brick Hasfield always said that of all the remedies that will not cure a cold, hot rum is the best.

More old-time medical advice from Grandma's library of life-saving hints:

Use oil of cinnamon to get rid of warts. Eat two lemons daily to reduce inflamatory rheumatism. Treat ailments of the kidneys with spinach and dandelion greens, soused with cider vinegar.

Make strong tea of elder blooms, add a third of sweet milk and soak a cloth for application upon sore eyes. For diarrhea, peel the inside bark of a sweet apple tree and drink the tea made by boiling it. Sprains can be relieved by applying a liniment made of the white of an egg and one tablespoon each of vinegar and turpentine.

Soak sore feet in water which has stood for at least two hours in wood ashes. If one has a cinder in an eye, rub the other eye vigorously and the irritated eye will feel no worse than the good one.

The best remedy for minor burns is a mixture of essence of peppermint and whiskey. Don't drink it, put it on the burns!

Rub teeth with soft cloth impregnated with chalk to get rid of tartar. To stop bleeding of a flesh wound, set woolen rags on fire and position the affected part in the smoke. If despondent, drink vinegar, a lot of it.

While not in her file, not to be forgotten is Grandma's emergency, life-preserving remedy for croup: A spoonful of human urine hourly until all danger is past!

Drastic? Yes, but anything that might work in the absence of the doctor, five miles and up to an hour and a half away, depending on the weather, is useful. As a youthful patient, we know about the croup treatment.

GRANDPA'S SOFA

If we were ever to layout a kitchen—which unfortunately we will not—we would certainly provide a strategic location for a rocking chair, exclusively for the man of the house.

Some folks practice the use of newfangled chairs which raise a man's feet higher than his head. There's nothing wrong with that; sometimes we wish our leaders had time for such repose so they could gather wisdom in peace and quiet.

On our grandparent's farm, the kitchen had an old sofa between the wall of a built-out nook and the cookstove; a warm, cozy spot claimed by Grandpa. But before dinner and on a Sunday afternoon his place of relaxation was in a kitchen rocking chair where, in the peacefulness of gentle motion, he could overhear feminine chit-chat and decide, if he must, his verdict on some family matters he sensed were arising.

Many women these days vote for small, efficient kitchens, with few steps between stove and sink, refrigerator and table, disposal and microwave. In our view, the trend should be to large roomy kitchens with ample space for a sofa behind the stove and a rocking chair for the stirring of good thoughts.

The Lady of Our House remembers her Perfect Day. We went to a restaurant that gave a 20 percent discount to Senior Citizens and the waiter deducted for her husband, but judged her too young to qualify! She's older!

★   ★   ★

CRUST TIME ON THE FARM

Crust time was fun time for youngsters on a farm, back when a motor-powered device to push you across snow-filled fields was but a gleam in some lonely inventor's eye.

An ice storm would coat the snow with a hard, slippery surface making footing treacherous on roads and paths, but turning hilly fields into speedways for downhill races and spills.

A heavy crust made it possible to walk on the snow, instead of plunging through it to fill felt boots to the top with snow quick to turn into dampness. It permitted traveling about a farm with impunity, searching for the slope of one's choice in winter's magical play.

It is the thing these days to put narrow boards on one's feet to traverse snow-covered territory. The closest we came to skis, at the young age of which we now speak, was a barrel stave on which Grandpa had fashioned a rude seat. This made a good vehicle for riding down hill, as long as one kept one's feet high in the air. Otherwise, a spill with dangerous possibilities.

We see youngsters today with store-bought plastic sheets or miniature bathtubs of the same stuff skimming over snow or crust. We did not know of these those many decades ago, but we had a suitable substitute. We are not speaking of sleds; favored was the lad with a Flexible Flyer. On crusts, sleds were dangerous and difficult to handle.

Our favorite and handy crust vehicle was a scoop shovel, the big kind used to transfer grain from bin to sack. Locating the shovel handle between one's high-held legs and hanging on to the handle firmly, one could sit on the concave steel shovel blade and take off down the hill, often to spin crazily around and around until the inevitable spill at the bottom.

The shovel blade became hot as it was massaged by the crust. One's rear could become more than warm. That was easily corrected by sitting on a burlap bag as a cushion. We couldn't get our feet high enough today!

★   ★   ★

TRAMPING THE LINES

When snow first came each year on Potato Hill, an old man and his grandson would "tramp the lines," an inspectior. of hedgerows and woods looking for animal tracks and other intelligence.

"It's time," he would say. That meant getting into felts and overs, a mackinaw coat and stocking cap, with mittens to match. We would walk down the lane from the barn to the "new ground," a partly-cleared lot, used both for lumbering and pasture. Then, a left turn, along a wide hedgerow dividing a swale from the back cornfield, along the potato patch, across the road to a full woodlot, through the woods to a pasture and around behind the house to the second orchard and the vineyard. You walked through the "first orchard" to go from house to barns.

Some of the route was part of our secret playground of non-winter days, where we would go scouting about, playing soldier or searching for woodchuck holes. Once, a chuck poked his nose out of his hole, about 10 feet away, chattered at us and sent us running, in youthful terror, for the house. Grandpa did not chide us for lack of courage.

There would be tracks in the snow, mostly of birds, squirrels and rabbits. Deer had not yet introduced themselves from Pennsylvania into that Southern Tier territory. The men folks of the Hill looked forward to annual hunting trips in the Adirondacks. Today deer are as plentiful on Potato Hill as in the Big Woods, even more, we'd guess, than around Fish Creek Club, on Tug Hill.

Once in a while, the old man would excitedly point to a footmark along the hedge and declare that a bobcat had been in the territory. "We'll have to tell Grandma to lock up her hens," he'd say.

We never knew if it was a bobcat, a domesticated cousin or a dog.

Years after, when Grandpa had gone on ahead, we saw a bobcat in the yard of our father's farm, up on the ridge above Potato Hill. We would never have expressed doubt of anything the old man said and we are happy we never even thought he might have been "making it all up."

You do not doubt one you love and trust.

★   ★   ★

CHRISTMAS WITHOUT TOYS

Twice we had no new toys for Christmas. We must have been three when Dad lost his job, and part of his eyesight, in a railroad accident. He was a fireman and relief engineer on the Lehigh Valley, running from Sayre, Pennsylvania, to Manchester, New York and back. After his engine derailed because someone failed to close a switch, and he couldn't pass a vision test, he was fired—no pension, no medical benefits, not even an extra week's pay.

The accident was just before Christmas. Perhaps it was lack of money that kept Mother and her young son from spending the holidays, as usual, with her parents on Potato Hill.

If we had been there, there would have been a toy, perhaps two or three, because Grandpa always made toys in his workshop. There was more hard luck that Christmas. Mother had a small savings account, but the bank closed and she lost her money. Dad was broke.

So we cried, Mother trying to comfort us as she always did, and Dad probably taking us aside to tell us to shape up and be a man. We didn't want to be a man, we wanted a new toy to play with—spoiled, selfish kid.

And that was not the only time. When we were six and with Grandpa and Grandma on Potato Hill, a neighbor's house burned the day before Christmas. Two little children from that large family came to stay with Grandma and Grandpa—and they gave two of my toys to them!

We cried again—according to family lore—resulting in a few taps on an appropriate place because Grandma wasn't one to put up with a little stinker without taking remedial action.

Life can be complicated when you are three and six.

Everyone at the circus was nervous as the lion tamer walked into the cage of snarling animals. All, that is, but a gray-haired woman who said, quietly, "I know how he feels. I drive a school bus."

WANT BABY: BURN APPLE WOOD

Now we go to the refrigerator during commercials, but in other days Grandpa saw to it that a young boy's before-bedtime needs were cared for. Apples, oyster crackers and often wild nuts, like black walnuts, hickories, even chestnuts, would maintain a youngster until the call for breakfast.

With the flames in the big parlor stove (it was in the living room) glowing through small isinglass windows, and sufficient room around the heater for all to keep warm, those before-bed minutes were happy times.

This is a different world today with automatic heat, moving pictures in a box and taken-for-granted electric lights. But there are some who can recall the round iron stove, the adjacent woodbox, papered on the exterior and battered within; the kerosene lamps, sometimes more for decoration than for illumination.

It got late those days around 7 in the evening; chore time was 6 in the morning. You could almost tell the time by Grandpa's departure for the cold cellar, to return with nuts and apples— Highland Beauties, Sheep Nose, Northern Spies, Pippins, Greenings, even Cabbage Heads. (Honest, that's an apple; we have never found one off Potato Hill.)

Grandpa might tell how he bought young apple trees off a roadside peddler and how the first one produced only one apple in its lifetime. And how he would laugh as he told about burning apple wood from that lazy tree.

"If you want a new baby in the house, burn apple wood," he'd say. "Maybe that accounts for you being here," looking straight at us.

In those days, we didn't know what he was talking about.

Brick Hasfield says the wife who drives from the front passenger seat is no worse than the husband who cooks from the dining room table.

GRANDPA'S GUN CONTROLS

The continuing fuss about gun controls reminds us of training in weapons safety when we were a youngster following Grandpa on armed tours of woods and hedgerows.

Grandma often objected when he would propose to take us on a hunting expedition, but he would declare that he had to do what he could to "make a man out of the little shaver."

There wasn't much to hunt on Potato Hill; rabbits, a few pheasants, but an ample supply of gray squirrels, few deer, once in a while a partridge. Today that region has its share of deer, the smaller Pennsylvania type that has migrated north since we were a child.

We have no memory of the make and vintage of Grandpa's double-barreled shotgun. Our uncle, some 15 years our senior, had a prized Winchester .32 Special, a single shot, octagon-barreled piece which, at the time, was regarded highly. We were sure it could shoot for miles.

Grandpa knew about guns, having carried a Spencer carbine as a Union cavalryman, as well as an issue pistol, one of which he brought home with him but which today we cannot name. In the war, he also lugged around a cavalryman's sword. His great granddaughter in Westernville has it on her wall.

At first, we had a wooden gun, whittled to scale by Grandpa during long winter evenings. Later, after we reached our "majority" at seven, and when we may have shown some signs of common sense, we were handed a wonderful vote of confidence—a Stevens, single shot .22 rifle.

We were given preliminary training and taken for a trial course in the woods. We wish we could report that we became a careful hunter in one day.

Grandpa shot a squirrel with his 12-gauge but we saw no moving targets. Finally, we could no longer resist the temptation and fired at a fence post from a reckless position to one side and close behind him. That ended our first armed episode in the field and possession of our .22 for a week.

Later we got our gun back, to undergo several lectures about safety as we tramped, unloaded, with Grandpa about the farm.

We had that Stevens rifle until we went away to prep school, after Grandpa had died, and then something happened to it. Probably Mother sold it at an auction in our absence. She shuddered every time she saw a gun.

Those were good days for a "little shaver" when he finally earned the privilege of going hunting with his Grandpa—.22 loaded! We have never been much of a hunter; it couldn't be much fun without that grand old man. We'd tramp the fields and hedgerows forever if we could go back and hear: "Let's see how you do with your gun."

Grandpa was willing for us to go along with him when he took the team to the blacksmith shop for new shoes. But, under pressure from Grandma, not when he took a cow to visit the neighbor's bull. We didn't know why until we were 10 or so. Left to him, Grandpa probably would have taken us; he believed life was to be lived, for young and old. But Grandma was determined to bring a little boy into manhood in a sweet, innocent setting.

The odds were too great for such noble ideals, especially on a farm.

BLOCKING OUT THE COLD

It could be harshly cold on Potato Hill. But we never thought much about it. The adults would note daily temperature readings, for conversational purposes, and go about their daily routine. All was low key in winter time, no field work, only feeding the stock and milking cows, wood chopping and every other day inspection of trap lines. Skunks, raccoons and muskrats were winter crops.

The farm house, built in the late 1860's, was prepared for winter in the last days of fall. Bales of straw were piled against the stone foundation walls, around front and side porches and over the outside cellar trap door. Grandma sniffed at the practice of some neighbors who used dry manure for insulation.

Wall cracks were filled with putty or by stuffing with pieces of newspaper. Old, handwoven rag rugs were handy for resisting drafts at the bottom of leaky doors. Wide cracks between door edges and casings were filled by tacking strips of cardboard in the cavities. Oiled paper was attached over most of the windows, especially in the rooms used in the winter. At least half of the house was shut off in the cold season.

There was no insulation, as we know it today, in the walls. Not in any of the dwellings on the hill. Grandma hung a colorful horse blanket on the wall back of the kitchen range where her man had a little nook for his napping couch. It was the warmest location in the house, one in which a young boy was not welcomed in the hours of rest desired by that kindly old man.

Firewood was plentiful, "worked up" in warmer times and cut to size for the kitchen range and the chunk stove in the living room. There was no shortage of kindling wood in the attached shed. One of our jobs was to keep the wood box full. It was built into the wall between kitchen and woodshed, with top openings in both places.

Grandma and Grandpa, all who shared the place with them, knew it took time and patience to live through the "Cold Time" on that wind-swept hill. The weather was not complained about; it was taken for granted.

They dressed their young grandson in long underwear, wool pants, flannel shirts, felts and overs and tucked him into bed wearing a long wool nightgown, under heavy blankets, atop a cornhusk mattress, in a room where the chunk stove pipe came through the floor on its way into a brick chimney opening. In severe weather, Grandma might warm the bed with hot coals in a pan on a stick or give the boy a hot water bottle.

The winters were chilly, but we did not notice.

Brick Hasfield says no matter how great a man is the size of his funeral will depend upon the weather.

A BOY FOR CRANK TURNING

Any man who looks back to his childhood on a farm in the early 1900's realizes that crank turning was a dominant feature of his young life. A boy close at hand was a candidate for turning the grindstone, the one-hole corn sheller, the turnip slicer or the cedar churn.

There was one crank that we were always eager to operate—that of the ice cream freezer.

Along about 4 in the afternoon of a blistering hot day, when a boy had been hoeing potatoes until the rows became twice as long, it was good to have Grandpa come along and say, "Well, young man, why don't you see if Grandma has a batch of ice cream ready to go."

If she was ready, the first task for the boy was to pull a cake of ice from the ice house, slosh the sawdust off in the milk trough, and pound the ice into small chunks in a burlap bag with the flat side of the axe.

The freezer can was filled with a mixture of rich cream, sugar and flavoring, usually vanilla, all combined in a session at the stove. Ice and salt were packed tightly around the can in the freezer. Then a boy began to turn.

At first, it was easy. Water ran from the little hole in the side of the apparatus and from time to time more crushed ice and salt were tamped around the round tub between the inner wall of the freezer and the can. Gradually it became harder to crank; the sweet mixture was thickening.

When it became almost impossible to turn any more, Grandma would test our endeavors by working the crank, 10 to 20 rounds, as if to show the boy he was delinquent in finishing his work. Then came the best of the job.

She would pull out the dasher and the boy cranker had the privilege of licking the paddles, after much of the ice cream had been pushed off by a knife into the can. Grandma understood her grandson; she left enough to remind her helper of the big dish that would be his after supper.

The job would not be completed until the freezer was "packed" and more ice put around the can to keep the contents in proper condition.

Some boy, grown into manhood, came up with the idea of having electricity do the turning. We have a freezer of each type in the cellar. Persuading grandkids to freeze ice cream the old-fashioned way can be difficult in these days of easy childhood. We still like the hand-cranked.

★   ★   ★

THE JANUARY THAW

The annual "January Thaw" on Potato Hill produced conditions that made living on a back country road in winter even more difficult.

The snow would wash from the hillsides; the dirt roads turned soft in the rains; sink holes appeared in low spots at the brooks which laced the grades. Good sleighing on hard packed snow was a blessing of winter.

When the "Thaw" came and the snow melted, as it always did sometime in January, Grandma would stay put in the house, nudging Grandpa or a young grandson to gather her eggs and feed chickens, ducks and the old tom turkey. Grandpa put aside his felts and overs for rubber boots and went to the barn to do chores or to putter in his shop.

Trips to the village, five miles away at the foot of the hill, were postponed during the "Thaw." But the district school went on; it took a blizzard to close the one-room institution. Muddy roads were no excuse. No shutting down at any time because school buses might slip and slide. There were no school buses.

Naps could be longer in "January Thaw" time, but we were not interested then in rest periods. Only Grandpa took advantage on his couch in the nook he had built for himself back of the kitchen range. Bad roads didn't bother him. He rested them out.

The "January Thaw"—capitalized because it was an annual event—could shut down the countryside until the rains ended, the runoffs stopped, the warm sun retreated and winter returned with a road-filling snowstorm.

★   ★   ★

BATH NIGHT

To a young boy who could see no virtue in any relationship between routine and cleanliness, Saturday night had an impact. It was "bath night" in our grandparents' farm house. Bath night, no matter what the temperature outside or how chilly the air coming under the door and through the cracks. It was the night you got out of long underwear and scrubbed.

The big wash tub rested in front of the kitchen stove, kettles of water were boiling on the range, the fire was stoked to the utmost limit of safety. No matter the outside temperature, it was warm in the kitchen—close to the stove.

Grandma had departed with stern warning that water was supposed to go on skin, not on her floor.

There were two approved methods. You could sit in the tub with knees drawn up around your chin or you could kneel. Either way, the process required a second party—Grandpa—to pour pails of hot water over lathered back, front and sides.

And when Grandpa took his bath—there was little modesty on a farm—it was the boy's turn to act like a shower; that word was not known on the hill. Grandpa required that his back be rubbed vigorously with a brush, an adult prerogative.

As a boy, we were never convinced of the necessity of taking a weekly bath. To us, it was risky business to get wet all over.

Brick Hasfield says an executive is a fellow who can take two hours for lunch and not be missed.

THE TIN PEDDLER

Anything out of the ordinary made an exciting day for a little fellow on a hillside farm. We have forgotten the name, never could pronounce it, of the semi-annual traveling peddler, a small rumpled man, driving a funny-looking wagon pulled by a sway-back horse. A store on wheels, with brooms, baskets, tin tubs and pails hanging on hooks on the exterior. It had hinged sides which opened to reveal lanterns, smaller tinware, spices, bolts of cloth (even lace) and, of course, needles, pins, thread and thimbles. He sold about everything a farm family might require, even out-dated magazines and farm publications given to him along his way and for which he asked two or three cents.

Sometimes he would stay overnight. After supper, the one we remember would take up his violin and play music we had never heard before, or after. "From the old country," Grandma said.

She called him "the notions man." Grandpa said he was a "tin peddler." We thought of him as a welcome adventurer, with a mysterious past in the world beyond the ridges, going from place to place, friendly and eager to talk, but with the sadness of cruel experience in his eyes.

He was a man of dignity, one who had escaped the evils of oppression to come to a land of opportunity. We heard him called names we did not understand; we liked him.

Enterprising merchants still sell from door to door, traveling in shiny trucks and elegant automobiles. But they do not carry with them the excitement of the tin peddler on those back country roads.

We remember him and his bag of hard candy from which came gifts for the young. He repaid for his lodging and meals with small articles of merchandise. He smiled at us.

Brick Hasfield says courting a girl is like dying, you have to do it for yourself.

FENCE-FIXIN' TIME

Early April was fence-fixin' time on Potato Hill. With the roads yet too muddy for easy travel, the days right after the snow disappeared were available for the annual mending of the field barriers.

The timing had to be proper, the ground could not be too spongy yet the frost had to have disappeared. On the appropriate day, Grandpa would hitch a horse to the stoneboat, load the necessary tools, sharpened fence posts and splicing wire and begin the fence patrol. We liked to be asked to come along. First, because we were invited to be with the old man we loved and second we would have the opportunity to feel important—by being asked to hold a new post in place while it was being driven into the ground.

Post holding was a sign of confidence in the man with the maul and the young grandson wanted, above all else, to show his trust. So he learned quickly never to flinch as Grandpa would come down, accurately, with a blow that drove a new cedar post into the half-frozen ground.

Fence fixin' is a springtime job, an annual inspection by all good farmers in a time of year when the weather is promising good days ahead and while it is yet too early to get on the fields to move soil around, preparatory to the annual seeding. It was a yearly task which stirred one's hopes for the good weather ahead.

Our Grandmother was not one to worry about past, present or future problems. She said: "Forget about who got the cat pregnant. Decide what we will do with the kittens."

SIMPLE LIFE, SIMPLE ATTIRE

Grandpa wore long underwear 365 days of the year. So did Grandma and a young grandson. It was the fashion in those days close to the last century when a bath once a week, on Saturday night, was held sufficient, even in fastidious circles.

We remember Grandma in long, dark, petticoated dresses, tight at the neck, almost sweeping the floor. Work attire was plain, her one concession an apron of gay colors.

The standard uniform, on that Potato Hill farm, for Grandpa and everyone of the male gender, big and little, was overalls—a loose, floppy article with drop seat, turned-up leg bottoms and shoulder straps holding up a bib front, no belt in the middle, big pockets on hips for red kerchiefs. Men would wear such to town; women wore "dresses."

Not to be forgotten is Grandma's black sunbonnet and how she wet her hair with black tea to keep it dark. And our one pair of overalls, one size lasted for several years, big at first, but easy to grow in.

A simple life and simple attire.

★　★　★

HILLSIDE BASEBALL

There was no ban on Sunday afternoon baseball on Potato Hill.

The home team was unique, not only in its losses, but also in the ages of its players, ranging between 10 and 70, if you count in Grandpa who would rather umpire.

We were too young to participate in his time, other than to hunt lost balls and carry water. Our fun, anticipated all week long, came from being the bat boy. The "gofer" we would be called today.

Later, in post-Grandpa days when we were in our teens, we had what our uncle called a "good hit, poor field" reputation. After all, errors were common on a diamond from which stones had to be picked before every game. We played in a prized pair of spiked shoes—originally designed for track events.

The diamond was laid out on a level section of the pasture behind the barn, with several large boulders entrenched in right field. Left field ran uphill.

That early Potato Hill team played with from six to nine men and boys, all the eligibles on the hill. An uncle pitched, a cousin caught. If the uncle gave up too may hits—scores were generally 21 to 18, 29 to 7 and the like—an eighth grader from a farm on the lower ridge would shift from the outfield and generally get clobbered.

The chief rival was an outfit from across the valley. We cannot remember ever beating them; they had two big sluggers and were not against bringing in ringers from other towns.

Our job of keeping track of balls was important. The team had only two or three badly scuffed ones and play stopped until any lost ball was found. No going home with foul balls in those days.

Except for sleigh rides in winter, baseball was the only organized fun on the hill. Everyone looked for Sunday, three or four hours on the diamond in the pasture or an occasional trip, by horse-drawn vehicles, to the home territory of another team.

We know the old country joke about sliding into a base which turned out to be evidence that cows had been grazing there. Not on our ball diamond. Removing such by long-handled shovel was part of the gofer's job, small as he was. We didn't "make" the team until after Grandpa's departure, when we may have been 12 or so. They tried to make a catcher out of us, with only a mask and a mitt, the umpire standing far back. But we had a bad habit of blinking our eyes when the batter swung and was soon shifted to third base.

Our best memory of baseball in those no-radio, no-TV days was the "big game" our uncle took us to in a nearby town equipped with a real ball park, bleachers, dugouts and such. There was a long rivalry between the local team—the best players in the whole county—and the Elmira Arctics, a charitable organization in the big city to the south which sponsored lots of things to raise money.

It seems, at that time, that the teams had split the first two games of a three-game series for a pot of $500 or more. The climax came after the big leagues closed their seasons. There was great excitement.

We did not know one player from another but our uncle was all worked up when the visiting pitcher was introduced as Smith or Jones or something like that, when he knew he was looking at Rube Marquard, famous big leaguer, from Boston, we think.

He quieted down when the locals' hurler turned out to be Lee Cadore, equally famous Brooklyn pitcher. The game ended in a one-run margin and we do not know who won.

Brick Hasfield says nothing depreciates a car faster than to have a neighbor buy a new one.

WAITING FOR MR. DAMON

It may be safely said that when one watches the clock for the arrival of the mailman retirement has set in. This did not apply to a young boy intensely attracted to the arrival of the RFD carrier many years ago on Potato Hill.

The most eagerly awaited visitor for us in those days was Mr. Damon, the mailman. He was the Monday through Saturday link to the outside world, in an era of no radio, no television and no telephone at our grandparents' place.

A single horse drew his enclosed light (box) buggy during the months of fair weather. Winter travel on his route (we never knew the exact distance) was with a team hitched to a light set of bobs, carrying an enclosure to protect against wind and snow.

It took mean weather to keep Mr. Damon from making his daily trip. He was as faithful as any, having been on his route since RFD service began in 1896.

He was a bachelor, a good situation for him because he did not have to worry about getting word back home if he was detained overnight by a sudden storm. He was welcomed at any place along his route, with shelter, grain for horses and food and bed for himself, never a charge. Mr. Damon did more than carry mail. He cheerfully performed errands for his patrons, some probably in violation of the rules.

His arrival was a happy moment for a young boy, even then fascinated by the printed word. Along with the daily newspaper from the big city 14 miles to the south—when Grandpa had sufficient money—there were the indispensible *Rural New Yorker*, *Hoard's Dairyman* and *American Agriculturist*. Grandma corresponded on postcards and received a fair number in return. We wish we had her collection.

One has to be older than their allotted years and to have lived as a child on a back country farm to know how anxiously we looked for Mr. Damon.

Brick Hasfield says the best substitute for brains is silence.

THE HOLD-UP MAN

Grandpa carried his cavalry pistol in a holster-pocket on the seat of his buggy. We were with him when he fired it at a stranger.

We must have been five or six when he took us to the big village at the foot of the lake, a great occasion, including a bag of peanuts and a motion picture show. We were coming back home in the dark, up the steep road which crossed the railroad tracks and curled around the side of the hill about two miles from the farm. We skirted the end of the lake and went up the dirt road which bore to the right, to lessen the grade, over the railroad crossing after a sharp left and then straight to the top of the second ridge, in sight of the farmhouse stark against the sky, on the third ridge. We could walk it, eyes closed, even now—but slowly.

The railroad attracted numerous hoboes who, when hungry would leave the freight cars and scour the countryside for a hand-out. Some were willing to chop wood for a meal, others simply begged. Grandma got more than her share of them, perhaps because of some secret sign on a fence post indicating a soft touch.

Anyway, as Grandpa drove across the tracks in the dusky evening, a man jumped out of a ditch and grabbed the horse by the bridle. Our Grandfather, in our eyes the bravest trooper of the Civil War, pulled his pistol from the holster on the seat and fired—hitting the horse in an ear, the animal bounding straight up the hill to the top of the ridge, nearly dropping from exhaustion.

The startled outlaw disappeared in the darkness.

Were we afraid? Never with Grandpa! We thought it was fun but Grandpa wouldn't talk about it. When the story got around, folks said he couldn't shoot straight, but sure knew how to get his horse's attention.

We've heard it said that at liberal weddings, the groom is holding the ring and the bride is holding the baby. And at conservative weddings, the old folks scoop the rice up from the sidewalk.

★   ★   ★

WATCH OUT FOR JOSHUA!

Winter was "puttering-around-time" for Grandpa. Grandma had full schedules every month of the year.

It was a season for Grandpa to go from job to job in his shop, for seasonable naps in the afternoon, to do the small indoor repairs put off in the "field work days."

He never stayed with one project long, as if he had an itch to move about and not get bogged down in uninteresting labor. He would sharpen a few cedar fence posts in a corner of the barn, then begin fixing a busted milk stool or repairing potato crates. He made his own crates with slats procured from a sawmill near the village. We wish we had a few of his new ones. They probably were worth a quarter or so in his day. We saw new ones, no better than his, tagged $10 recently.

Best of all, he liked to tinker around his forge. He had a small, but sufficient blacksmithing corner in the shop and did minor iron work. He shoed his own horses.

We had a job in the shop—sweeping out. There we were taught to be thorough and to persist until the work was done. We never liked sweeping out the granary, that room with tin over knot holes and cracks to keep rodents out.

Grandpa always warned us: "Watch out for Old Joshua, that big rat that's been around for years, stealing my grain. We know each other well; he may bite you!"

Strange—we never saw Old Joshua.

THE BABY AND THE STORM

We were not around when this happened so we must rely upon several versions of a family tale handed down from generation to generation.

Grandpa was not one to be excited about snowstorms. He simply dug his way to the barn, took care of the stock and retired to his couch behind the kitchen wood stove to let the storm blow itself out.

There was an exception, a happening told at family gatherings.

Late one winter afternoon, with dark clouds on the horizon, a neighbor came to Grandpa's house for help—his wife was about to deliver.

Grandpa put on his woolen pants and mackinaw coat, pulled on boots over his felts and took up his fur hat. He hitched the road horse to the Portland cutter, took Grandma to the neighbor's house and set off for the village, five miles away, to get Dr. Bond, the reliable country physician who made house calls in all kinds of weather. There was no telephone system then on Potato Hill.

The doctor was located about dark, on another case, and started out with Grandpa on the trip to help the expectant woman on the second ridge above Potato Hill. Suddenly a storm broke and visibility disappeared in swirling snow that began piling up unseen drifts. The horse, built more for speed than endurance, did the best it could before stopping, exhausted. Grandpa had lived his life with snow and horses, even in Union cavalry in the stormy mountains of what is now West Virginia. He was not a man to panic.

Grandpa unhitched the horse, took it by the bridle and found his way to a hedgerow. There he hitched the horse, secured a blanket from the cutter and tied it around the animal with the reins.

Then he tipped the cutter over as a windbreak against the snow-filled wind, wrapped the doctor, who was not young, in the second blanket and, clasping the physician in his arms, pulled the buffalo robe around the two of them. No one ventured on the road in winter, in those days, without at least two blankets, the buffalo robe and one for the horse.

Dr. Bond produced an emergency contribution, it was said, a supply of whiskey from his medicine bag, and the two spent the rest of the night the best they could, surviving without lasting damage.

When visibility came in the morning they found they were less than 200 yards from their destination, a fact, it is related, that both irritated and humored Grandpa.

The patient? Apparently she was feeling fine when unneeded medical help arrived. We wonder if she named the baby after Dr. Bond or Grandpa.

THE TRACKS SANTA LEFT

If we could wave a magic wand and have one wish come true: To be again at Christmas time on Grandpa's and Grandma's farm.

It was a dirt road place five miles from the village, high on Potato Hill in Schuyler County, overlooking beautiful Seneca Lake. Five miles in those days was a long way in winter, with roads often blocked by snow drifts and the bobsled team striking off across the fields.

Grandpa did certain things at Christmas, the same way, year after year. So two days before Christmas, he hitched the team to the bobs, lifted the young grandson aboard and drove to the lower woods. There was the tree, at least seven feet high and well shaped.

Grandma, too, as Grandmas always do, began thinking of Christmas long before. Looking back, we know the charm of Christmas on that back country farm was in the self-reliance of the family.

Grandma had no electric Christmas lights, tinsel or glass ornaments, except for a few decorations she had purchased when she went to Niagara Falls or to Oregon on a cross-continent train, her only two long trips away from home. She made her own candy canes, strung long strings of cranberries and colored popcorn, decked the tree in tiny red ribbons and hung cookies, shaped like stars and trees and elves, each from her oven.

There would be only one candle on the tree, at the very top, and that lit only for a few minutes on Christmas Eve. Grandma made the candle. They probably didn't have more than $400 cash money all year but they had plenty of other things, including a great love.

Hams and bacon slabs hung in the smokehouse, there were apples in cellar bins, flour from their wheat, horses, cows and sheep in the barn, chickens in the henhouse, vegetables and nuts stored away. Shelves were stacked with canned food and over in a dark corner Grandma's elderberry wine. And two big barrels of hard cider Grandpa drew on when neighbors came.

They were wealthy in the fruits of their land, which they had cleared and on which they had built their home, on top of that windy ridge, when Grandpa returned from the Civil War.

The farmhouse had many mysteries for a three-year-old. There was an old suction pump by the sink in the kitchen, a wood box that filled from the woodshed but opened into the kitchen, and a big horsehair couch behind the kitchen stove, for Grandpa's nap.

We were never permitted alone in the unheated parlor, filled with eye-catching things. Mother had been married there, she said, and we saw an uncle buried from there.

Grandma and Grandpa lived in the kitchen, the long, narrow dining room, the cold bedrooms, and the living room heated by a big chunk stove with small isinglass windows. The heat on a cold night was in direct proportion to one's distance from the stove.

Come Christmas Eve, the family gathered in front of the tree in the corner. There were no presents in sight. But there always were when a grandson got up early the next morning. Not many, perhaps a game from his parents, a pair of skis Grandpa had made from barrel staves, and little homemade things from Santa Claus. His other name was Grandma.

Christmas songs were played on the Edison phonograph, with big painted horn and cylinder records. Mother would go to the pump organ and the family would sing about the Babe whose birthday it would be.

Grandma would supervise a collection of popcorn, apples, sweet cider and all the walnut, butternut and hickory nuts you could crack, using a hammer and one of her old irons.

When it got late, about 9, Grandpa would stand, all would be quiet and he'd say a prayer of thanks for all the goodness, ending with a request for continued blessings. Then he would take the boy by the hand, help him put on felts and overs, and they would tramp through the snow to the barn.

When he rolled back the big door you could see steam rising from the noses of the stock. Grandpa would give another feeding to the horses, the cows, pigs and sheep. "It's Christmas for them, too," he'd say.

As the two walked back to the house, Grandpa would wonder out loud—about what direction Santa Claus would come, whether anyone would see his tracks the next morning, and wasn't it too bad the reindeer couldn't draw the sleigh up the hill? Seemed Santa Claus would have to use horses.

The three-year-older would wonder, too, as he was taken to bed in a big, cold, upstairs room, warm under three blankets atop a sheet on a mattress filled with crinkling corn husks. Grandma had warmed the nest with a bed warmer.

As he wondered, he'd try to match the wallpaper squares, the room lighted by a lamp Grandma left lit on a dresser until one fell asleep.

Grandma had papered the room out of sample wallpaper books. We never found a single one of the 18-inch squares that matched, on walls or ceiling.

After midnight when all was quiet downstairs and disregarding strict instructions to stay in bed until called, the boy tiptoed in bare feet and flannel nightgown, down the stairs to see if Santa Claus had come.

As he turned the corner from the foot of the stairs into the living room, he was startled to see—not Santa Claus but his grandfather, in nightgown and cap, alone in his rocking chair, before the parlor stove in which a fresh chunk was giving off sparks that shown through small isinglass windows to dimly illuminate the room.

The old man—he was nearly 75—motioned the boy to his side, said nothing, placed him on his knee and held him tight. The two watched the fire for precious minutes, until the grandfather put the boy on his feet and walked him, hand in hand, up the stairs to his bed. Not a word was spoken.

Santa Claus had come, the boy could see something in a black stocking hanging on a chair over by the stove. But, so had the unspoken affinity between man and child increased in warmth, although then we did not know how cherished those tender moments would become.

Come six in the morning, Grandpa would pound on the ceiling of the living room below with the end of the broom. Out the boy would tumble, pulling on his clothes in the cold and with Grandpa go looking for Santa Claus' tracks.

They were there!

One year they were in the snow across the backyard and up to the woodshed door, the next year across the front yard to the front door. We always were too excited in those priceless short years to follow them back.

If we had, we know now they could have led to the barn because Grandpa went out every Christmas Eve, after his grandson had gone to bed, hitched the team to the bobsled and made the tracks for Santa Claus—and a little boy.

★   ★   ★

THE VILLAGE BARBER SHOP

The barber shop in the village at the foot of Potato Hill was the community club for males. Women had church groups and the Grange Hall was for gatherings of mixed character. The barber shop was the listening post for community reports and male conversation, a constant topic being the weather. Grandma said men gossiped there. Grandpa quietly denied any such, men talked things over.

She insisted Grandpa stay with us while on visits to the barber shop. She may have heard that topics not for a youngster's ears were discussed or she may have been apprehensive that her grandson might come to her for an explanation of a new word he had heard. That never happened. If needed, such assistance could be secured from Grandpa. He was outspoken.

Or Grandma may have heard reports of a certain art form that decorated a wall in that shop, behind a screen. When we were a little fellow we thought that all ladies of the outside world were like those in that picture—big and wearing red tights.

Grandpa didn't always mind his wife. He would leave us waiting our turn with the barber while he went about his business. We liked that. It gave the opportunity to search through strange magazines. Grandma would have objected to some of those pictures, too, but we were too young to be inspired.

The barber was also the town undertaker. When the infrequent call came for such services, he drew the shades of his shop—a signal of a death in the community. He also operated the furniture store next door.

His one chair was bright and shiny in leather and chrome. It swung around in front of a big mirror, bordered with cubby holes sheltering individual shaving mugs. Fancy bottles of colored hair tonics and face lotions lined the shelf. The barber shop smelled good.

There was no wireless news, the paper came out once a week. Even so, the news was not dated in that shop and was well debated, from latest comings and goings to who had been caught at something worth comment.

There was a revolving red and white striped pole in front, encased in a glass tube. Don't hold us to statistics, but we think a haircut was 15 cents, a shampoo a dime and a shave, with hot towel and lotion, 20 cents. The barber lanced boils and exploded pimples without charge.

Men once farm boys know about razor straps, suitable appliances for punishment of youngsters requiring a good bringing up. One hung on the barber's chair. He'd hone his straight razor, pull a hair from his head and cut it without the hair bending.

Neatness in male appearance was maintained, weighty topics fairly debated and collective judgments passed in that barber shop. We grew almost to manhood within its protection.

The barber we knew was a wise man, an arbiter of disputes, a presiding judge of debates, a man who kept his personal counsel and left unassailable opinions to his customers. The old barber shop has gone the way of the one-horse cultivator, the barrel churn, the hand pump in the kitchen and the milking stool.

Try getting a shave today, at almost any price.

Brick Hasfield says the best way to get rid of weeds is to sell the place.

THE PREACHER'S "NAUGHTY WORDS"

Once a local minister offered to write an editorial if we would preach a sermon. We declined; we would not be at home in a pulpit and we lacked the elementary advantages of Sunday School.

Grandpa read his Bible many evenings in the sancity of his

home, but the family did not travel the 10 miles to and from the church in the village every Sunday. When such absence had been too long for the happiness of Grandma, she would decree the hour down, hour or more back horse-power trip.

There was no Sunday School in their church and a young child sat quietly, as he was taught, and dreamed of picking wintergreen berries or looking for bee trees with an uncle. It was a long sit. The man in dark clothes up on the platform had little meaning for a child. Particularly when what he said was confusing.

Grandma always reminded us to forget the naughty words Grandpa said when he hit his thumb with a hammer or when the team geed instead of hawed. But the preacher said the same words and Grandma listened quietly! We didn't understand until we grew older and went to church more willingly—because, in a small village, that was where the girls were!

Then, of course, we grew out of that and, under the influence of another devoted woman, came to look forward to going to church —with an understanding of the true meaning and significance of the words that were naughty when said by Grandpa.

★   ★   ★

FIREWATER FROZE?

This report was repeated, year after year, on Potato Hill.

Seems that an Indian went on the coldest day of winter to the village tavern, lingering around the stove in the barroom for hours while imbibing freely of firewater.

Finally, he started up the hill for his place in Texas Hollow, but was found dead along the way, frozen to death. Some of his friends held an inquest and decided that the tavern keeper was to be held liable for the sudden departure to the happy hunting grounds. They insisted that the bartender had watered his whiskey so much, as was his known practice with Indian trade, that the water froze in the victim's stomach and killed him.

Could be true, but there were no Indians on Potato Hill or in Texas Hollow.

★   ★   ★

WHIPPING THE NUT TREES

There came a time every year to "whip" the nut trees.

Every well-sustained farm family in the days we knew long ago was prepared for winter with ample supplies of nuts, along with apples, sauerkraut, home canned goods, jams, jellies, hams and bacon.

The women of the house put up and stored most of the provisions for a long season. Gathering nuts was a job for the menfolk —aided by young boys and girls.

Around house-banking, woodshed-filling-time, Grandpa looked forward to a sunny afternoon for collecting the year's supply of nuts. They were a significant part of the family diet, particularly just before bedtime. A few pints of any variety were insufficient for a long winter. The nuts in the store room were kept in bushel crates lined with burlap and filled with chestnuts, walnuts, hickory and butternuts. The chestnut trees are gone now, victims of a wide sweeping disease; in our childhood they were healthy and productive.

Wild nuts take their own time in dropping, their mission to unite with rich soil to keep the variety alive. Gathering nuts meant making reluctant branches release their crop before its time.

That's where the "whipping" comes in. Those expert in gathering the tasty crop had long, limber sticks, like a stripped branch eight or more feet long, with which to lash the trees as far up as one could reach.

Young grandkids helped by throwing short pieces of wood, broken branches and such into the trees, hoping to loosen clusters of nuts. Never was a tree cleanly picked of its treasure, even by expert grandfathers.

Before this operation began, horse blankets were laid under the trees, to catch the fallen harvest, thus preventing nuts from hiding in tall grasses.

It was worth all the trouble because without the yearly supply from the trees in the hedgerows, there would not have been good times around the living room stove on nights when the winds moaned about the corners of the house and the clapboards creaked in below-zero weather.

Sitting on a stool with a gunny sack on one's lap, an old flatiron between the knees and a hammer in hand, with an assortment of black walnuts, chestnuts, hickories and butternuts in a dish alongside, was part of life on Potato Hill.

Brick Hasfield says a practical nurse is one who marries a rich patient.

SNOW, SNOW, SNOW

In winters seven decades and more ago, the amount, kind and duration of snow on Potato Hill was vital knowledge. There was no snow plowing as we know it now; a blizzard might isolate back road farm families for days.

Rural citizens of those times liked a covering of snow on the roads, about six inches deep, of a type that packed down for easy passage of cutters and sleighs.

Six, eight, ten inches of new snow, accompanied by high winds, could produce heavy drift blockades, which often had to be opened to passage by shoveling one-track lanes. These filled in again with every new wind.

Often drifts would be bypassed by leaving the road and driving over open fields, a common practice sometimes made legal by local laws which overrode property owners' objections.

Our grandfather joined with his neighbors in rolling winter roads, using a two-team hitch on a large wooden snowroller, the board cylinder higher than a tall man. This produced good sleighing, but in the spring left ribbons of dirty snow on roads which remained impassable until the rising sun ended the problem. Springtime could be more difficult for travel than winter; in early spring dirt roads were sloppy, the fields, where used, often very muddy.

Along with observations about the weather, a favorite topic of winter conversation, as we dimly remember, was the broad subject of sleighing conditions, classified as good, so-so and bad. Good meant the roads were open and well covered with snow, no big drifts or bare spots. A road horse would have no difficulty pulling a cutter along at a steady clip. Bad was just that, difficult for man and beast, changeable from day to day, with hopes high for a light storm. So-so covered all conditions in between.

Moving snow about may be fun, for a while, especially if you have one of those metal devices that blows the stuff to one side or another. But on Potato Hill, before the days of such mechanized apparatus, shoveling snow was not something to look at with anticipation. To be maintained were paths from the house to the barns, from the house to the chicken coop, from the house to the pig pen and first on the list, from the house to the privy behind the wood shed.

Why the latter priority, we'll never know precisely because at our grandparents' place the "necessary" was an integral part of the wood shed, approached on a board walk, from the back kitchen door. The outside privy was for summer use. Grandma wasn't given to levity but, according to our Mother, she once joked that the outside path was merely an emergency measure, in case of an overcrowded situation.

A farm boy might like to wallow in snow, forming a passable trail. But adults had grown out of such traits and demanded a wide, clean path through the white banks.

Grandpa would take pity if the show was heavy and deep, hitching a horse to a homemade contraption of two heavy planks, braced so as to form a stout V. That was his kind of a snow plow, not a blower but heavy enough to do the job, provided man and boy rode the apparatus to keep it to its business.

The patient looked up from the operating table and asked why all the shades were drawn.

"There's a fire across the street," his doctor said, "and I don't want you to wake up and think the operation was a failure."

BROOM OUTSIDE THE DOOR

Winter was the time for the broom Grandma kept outside her kitchen door.

It was not for decoration. All who entered were reminded to use it—"brush off the snow and slush on your boots!" A little boy, often inattentive in his rush for the cookie jar, received personal attention.

Only after boots were clean was one privileged to walk into a small, enclosed space called the storm shed, a portable structure erected each winter to form a leaky air lock, and there remove his "overs," low two- or three-hook rubber boots covering his "felts." The latter were stiff felt stockings, open at the top (for snow to drop in, we thought) and capable of use as slippers. They were knee high and warm. On that farm, young and old lived in felt boots during waking hours in winter.

"Felts and overs," a broom outside the door, Grandma's place.

Once upon a time, a new automobile could be bought for under $500, a good suit of men's clothes for under $40, boys looked different than girls and today's politicians were unborn.

GRANDMA'S CHICKENS

Grandpa said the chickens were the responsibility of his five-year-old grandson. He was always kidding.

The chickens belonged to Grandma. She even kept a small shotgun handy in case a four-footed marauder caused a sudden fuss in her flock.

Her coop was the only colorful structure on that farm, red with a white stripe and located midway, off the path, between house and barn. The "run," a large wire pen, was attached to one side, covered with wire to keep hawks from swooping down for a meal.

The chickens "ranged" in warm months, being given freedom of barns, yards and the woods across the road. They would not wander off; chickens are not bright, but hers knew where the daily meal was scattered.

There was no scientific management of that Potato Hill flock. Grandma had Rhode Island Reds, and their cousins, Plymouth Rocks, New Hampshires, good for meaty Sunday dinners, and the egg-producing champs of her time, White Leghorns. With farm roosters, paying no attention to the sacredness of the strain, the blood lines of her chickens were never permanent.

She had one old New Hampshire rooster who had only the assistance of an apprentice, a scared White Leghorn male. Scared because the old boy did not appreciate whatever help the young Leghorn could provide and who always chased the youngster away from the hens that caught his eye.

That problem finally was solved. After the Leghorn became more confident. Grandma had the old rooster for Sunday dinner, probably in a stew for he was an old-timer.

Brick Hasfield says don't try keeping up with the Joneses unless you know where they are going.

GRANDMA'S SALAD ROW

The first seeds Grandma planted in her garden went into her "salad row." You can read about "broad row" gardening in modern magazines, as if it is something new. To her it was just common sense to plant garden seeds with various kinds mixed together instead of in single rows where weeds have more than an even chance. Besides, it was a practice handed down from her mother, something to be followed, generation by generation, even ours.

She would size out a broad row across her garden, to one side of the wood shed, about one and a half times the width of her rake. She would add sufficient dry manure and a considerable amount of sand, hilling the mixture into a deep, raised bed, long in length, walkways on both sides.

The seeds she had saved from last season—radish, lettuce, beet, carrot, chard, spinach—were mixed in a cup and sprinkled thickly over the bed. Then she would rake them into the ground, tamping slightly. This was early in the season, mid-April for sure, if the rains held off.

These were cold weather seeds, to be planted as soon as the soil could be worked, as soon as a ball of earth crumbled when packed in a hand. She knew that certain other seeds, like sweet corn, squash, beans and melons would "just sit there" if planted early. She had patience and knowledge, always sowing sweet peas on Good Friday and never planting potatoes until the full of the moon.

Her "salad row" came up like a torrent, springing from the ground. When the first of the mixed vegetables were nearing half an inch high, she would take her rake and pull it carefully through the thick growth, from side to side. She was cold-hearted about this procedure.

Not only did she rake out a lot of the multitude of young plants, she never walked by the bed without reaching down for handfuls of vegetation. Even so, the growth was sufficient to smother the weeds and give the remaining plants a good chance for maturity.

Radishes, of course, came first. She pulled them daily until they were no more, a thinning in itself. She never picked lettuce, leaf by leaf; she pulled up whole plants. The idea was simple, to provide sufficient breathing space even if one had to destroy good vegetable plants. She put newspapers on the walkways around the bed, held in place by soil around the edges. With that her weed problem was solved and her "salad row" a success.

We can prove it works in our garden, in a vegetable bed that is a living testimonial to a wise old lady of Potato Hill.

Brick Hasfield says no athlete should be awarded a diploma unless he can read it.

YOU SHOULD TRY SWITCHEL

Ask any one-time farm boy, now retired from years in a city job, and you are likely to find he's well acquainted with switchel, perhaps agriculture's best known hot weather drink.

There are several recipes, each with very staunch enthusiasts. Grandma used a gallon of water, two cups of white sugar, a cup of molasses, a cup and a quarter of vinegar, a heaping teaspoon of ginger and, for smoothness, a good handful of rolled oats. Mother substituted brown sugar for the white and increased the allotment of vinegar.

Even if we used Grandma's recipe without deviation, we could never produce the switchel she served her menfolk in the hay field on a hot summer day. We do not have a spring house in which to place the switchel jugs in cool, running water.

As to "the most important part," as suggested by a novice in this activity, Grandma would never permit the use of rum. But it's an idea with merit.

A customer bought baby clothes at a store, a clerk asking: "Expecting?" "No," said the buyer, "I'm sure."

BEANS AND POTATOES

Our grandfather did not have a silo on his Potato Hill farm. His dairy herd was never more than six milch cows. The bull was available at a neighbor's place.

He had an old corn chopper, powered by a portable engine on skids, one or two cylinders, we've forgotten. It made a "put-put-put" sound we can still hear.

The chopper sliced corn stalks into an interior corner of the barn, above the winter quarters of the cows. Grandpa fed the silage first, then resorted to hay and a little grain, hoping to have enough to carry his herd and his horses over a long winter. Before spring, they must have been aching for the pasture field.

Bean harvesting was a dirty job, uprooting vines with dried pods loaded with hard beans, the kind used for routine Saturday night meals. The bean digger pulled them with dirt clinging to the roots. Then they were fed through the threshing machine, stationed in the field, the empty vines being deposited in a fog of dust, for spreading on the field. In days before a threshing machine was available, bean vines were flailed on the barn floor, a very long and weary job.

Grandpa did not speculate in beans, as did our father in later years. We recall that Dad had a good five-acre crop which, at seven cents a pound, produced a fair profit. So, being an instant agricultural economist, he planted 10 acres of beans the following year, a practice others of like wisdom must have followed because beans sold for three cents a pound that following year.

Digging potatoes required stoop labor, considered by adults highly suitable for youngsters—picking up tubers dug by horse-drawn machine from their nests in the ground and putting them into shoulder sacks for transport to strategically placed crates.

We recall that one year potatoes were so cheap it did not pay to haul them to the village railroad station for shipment to market. So Dad bought extra pigs and fed them raw potatoes.

At our prep school reunions, we noticed that the fellow who generally was late for class was first at the bar.

GRANDMA'S LILACS

She was a young bride when she planted the small bushes in the rear yard of the unfinished farmhouse she and her man were building high up on the eastern hill overlooking Seneca Lake.

She became our maternal grandmother and her lilacs bloomed for more than 100 years. They bore those old-fashioned purple blooms which brought fragrance to a May day until a few years ago when all trace of the old homestead was wiped out, lilacs and all. Grandpa would probably have approved of increasing the usable tillable land, now that the house was destroyed by fire, but Grandma would have wiped a tear with her gingham apron.

How lucky we have been to go back when the lilacs were blooming. They were colorful evidence of a woman's faith in marriage and the land. Lilacs have a meaningful place in our history. Grandma's have been special to this boy turned man with precious memories.

WET MITTENS ON THE STOVE

There was a lingering smell in Grandma's kitchen not associated with her new bread, cookies, cakes or pies or open stock pot on the back of the stove. Those were good smells, but the one that persists was the faint but persistent scent of wet woolen mittens and damp felt boots slightly steaming on the drying rods of the wood-burning kitchen stove.

Grandpa hand-fastened small iron rods that swung out from the collar around the stovepipe for strategic placement over the hot spots of the range. Those whose wet mittens and felt boots were dried in this fashion will sniff and remember.

Brick Hasfield says the average time between throwing something out and needing it again is about two weeks.

REPUBLICANS MADE GRANDMA CRY

We were too young to know, but we pass along a family political hand-down, as told to us by our Mother.

The folks on Potato Hill, not just Grandpa and Grandma, but all the adults up and down the roads that passed over and along the big ridge, were Democrats. Only the men voted, but the women were persuasive.

Not big city Democrats; Grandpa and Grandma may never have heard of Tammany Hall. They were farmer Democrats, faithful followers of William Jennings Bryan, Grover Cleveland and Woodrow Wilson. They saw Republicans as rich city folks who cared little for common people. Grandpa didn't fight in the Civil War for Abraham Lincoln and the Republicans; he went to war for his country and voted old line Democratic.

We remember the tears in Grandma's eyes when a Republican succeeded Wilson in the White House. But, by the way he talked, Grandpa may have voted for Teddy Roosevelt, for whom he had vocal admiration.

★　★　★

A BOY GOES TO TOWN

The important days of our young life were those when Grandpa would say, "We are going to the village, want to go along?" It didn't take a six-year-old long to make up his mind, even if Grandma insisted we would have to "wash your face and hands and behind your ears."

Going to the village was a five-mile horse and buggy trip, one way. Down the big hill by the one-room school house and across the flats at the bottom of the hill, then over the railroad bridge into the settlement around five roads meeting at a common center. It may have had 200 residents, counting those living out their retirement days from farms their sons tilled and those who had steady jobs in the grist mill, with the railroad, at the school, the chair factory and the grocery and hardware establishments.

The main street, if it could be so called, led past the barber shop, two grocery stores, the post office, a small eating place, a not-very-busy inn without a bar and a Grange Hall. Two churches, Methodist and Presbyterian, served the religious.

People did not hurry on that street. They strolled, the women in dresses so long they swept the ground, causing the wearers to gather their skirts in hand just enough so that they did not trail in the dirt. Little girls had dresses that reached far below their knees, their hair in curls or braids tied with big bows. They walked demurely beside their mothers, carrying little crocheted or beaded bags.

Little boys wore long black stockings and short pants, their shirts open at the neck, with long sleeves to the wrist. All the men wore hats, as did their ladies.

The grocer, presiding over the store where the board sidewalk was lined with bushel baskets and crates of produce, was in shirt-sleeves and vest with a big white apron tied around his middle. He sometimes stood in the doorway, talking to passersby.

There were hitching posts and rails all along the store section and, with no one to keep the street clean, as in big cities, there was that peculiar odor of the society of horse and man.

Once in a while, something called an automobile would pass rapidly—perhaps 10 miles an hour. The driver usually wore a duster, cap and goggles and most everyone rushed to windows or doorways to see the new mechanical device.

The automobile did not yet cause as much attention as a runaway horse or team. That was real excitement, for a maddened horse dashing down the road out of control, dragging an often damaged buggy or wagon, could create a very dangerous situation.

Life in 1910 was not dull, not on those days when a little boy had the privilege of going to the village with his grandparents.

You can tell when our favorite preachers at our weekly luncheon club are hungry. Their blessings are shorter.

"WATCHING COWS" DUTY

Once we were big enough to walk along a hedgerow all by ourself, looking for animal holes, we were old enough to "watch cows," assisted by Shep, the dog.

Grandpa's hay fields were not fenced and when, after cutting, he wished to give the cows a treat, he would turn them out on the open field and delegate to his small grandson the grave responsibility of keeping them out of the adjacent corn field.

It did not matter if they wandered into the dirt road running along one side; all traffic was non-motorized. All the youngster had to accomplish was to keep the bovines in the new-cut area. And out of the corn! And no throwing stones to enforce commands!

Generally, all went well for about half an hour and then old Bess, the matron of the herd, would start to drift over toward the corn. Shep would be off on an exploring adventure of his own, sniffing at any promising smells that arose from holes and stumps.

Then it began, as it always began. The young boy would go after Bess and begin driving her back toward the main body of the herd. As this was progressing, another cow would make a slow break for the cornfield. Then another and another.

Suddenly, a small boy had three or four cows deciding to go their own way, as long as it led to the green crop in the next field. No dreaming then about adventures to come in manhood; and no obedience of the "no stones" rule. Small gravel by the handful helped get a cow's attention.

The more one ran about, like a watch dog, the more the cows would scatter. Then Shep would come back on the job and help round up the strays. This would go on until the farm bell rang, a signal to bring the cows to the barn. Come to think of it, we never liked "watching cows."

Brick Hasfield says never weigh yourself when you are feeling blue.

THE COUNTRY STORE

A dwindling segment of the population is familiar with the old country store; more have some knowledge gained from viewing lifeless replicas at tourist attraction "villages."

The country store in the village, off the hill, was the supply point for the few staples unattainable from the farm, Grandma trading eggs for salt, pepper, coffee and the like. It was also headquarters for friendly conversation, a listening post which spread the joys and sorrows of a wide community.

We remember two aspects of the country store—its smell and its candy counter. Where else would there be such an exhilarating aroma as that mixture of fresh-ground coffee blended with nostril-filling scents of dill pickles, spiced with the odors of rat cheese, salt codfish, hanging bacon slabs and open barrels of molasses? Add the smell of fertilizer, the odor of kerosene, the tantalizing appeal of dark chocolate and the subtle scent of wool clothes on the racks.

The combined smell of the country store! It is nostalgic now; we probably paid scant attention in our hurry to get to the candy displays. There, with a few pennies, we could ponder a weighty choice of early life—chocolate drops, hard sugars, sweet sticks, licorice or gum? This demanded close attention. What pennies could buy then made decisions mind-gripping.

What we need today is the production of the smell of the old country store. It would sell!

Brick Hasfield says parents should realize, in these times, that a boy's attention to plants in his bedroom does not necessarily mean he is intending to be a botanist.

THE MAGIC TIME

Indian Summer? Some folks insist on designating any nice day in late September or early October as the beginning of that brief, but fabulous period which does not generally come until November.

You can get many answers as to Indian Summer, generally said to be a spell of delightful weather, a farewell to Summer, the last grand days before Winter. We went to the Old Farmer's Almanac for wisdom, learning that the weather must be warm, the wind must be still, the barometer high and the nights clear and chilly. Above all, a smoky haze must permeate the atmosphere.

Most will accept that definition, so anxious are they for what can be one of the wonderful times of the year. But they quarrel about the timing of the annual blessing, some declaring there is a stated period of Year's schedule, others insisting there is no such regularity.

We'll take Grandpa's word for it. Indian Summer, we learned at his feet, comes after a hard frost and a spell of cold weather. It simply isn't Indian Summer if these have not occurred.

Those who follow charts, like in the Almanac, go by the saying: "If All Saints brings out Winter, St. Martin's brings out Indian Summer." For those only slightly interested, St. Martin's Day coincides with Veterans' Day, November 11. The rigid in this matter declare that Indian Summer must come between November 11 and November 20 and if it does not occur in this span, the year is devoid of such a gift.

The old man who gave us our first taste of knowledge said that it was a time when a young boy could look at a hazy field of stacked cornstalks and see Indians dancing in campfire smoke around wigwams.

★   ★   ★

BEWARE OF PUMPKINS

There are those who insist that when the heat is searing you can hear the corn growing. Stand on the edge of a corn field in a hushed late afternoon and listen, they suggest, for the faint rustle of the leaves as the stalks reach out for their ordered destiny.

Not according to Grandpa. He told us: "Lad, see those pumpkin vines among the corn in that field? Never walk alone down those rows. What some folks say about hearing corn growing is the pumpkin vines reaching out to trap a little boy. They twine their tentacles around him and pin him to the ground. What you hear is not the corn growing, it's the pumpkins looking for a young lad. Remember that!"

To this day, we would never entertain the thought of walking in a full-grown pumpkin patch.

TRACKIN' COULD BE SCARY

We cannot tell one animal or bird track in the snow from another. It is the fault of our Grandfather.

When we were a little guy, come the first snow and he would say: "We are going trackin'." Those were the very early days, before he entrusted us with a single-shot .22 rifle and took us squirrel hunting. "Trackin'" was an unarmed educational course in the woods. It was as if he was taking inventory of the wildlife in his territory. It was also a time to have fun with a young, gullible grandson.

"Look," he'd say, "a lot of squirrels around here." Or, down by the swamp, pointing to a track punctuated by a dragging tail, "that may be a beaver." He could have told us it was an otter, a weasel, a mink or a skunk.

We believed him when he pointed to a big track, probably a dog's, and said, "Let's get out of here, that could be a wildcat." Trackin' could be scary for a boy who rightly believed everything his best friend said.

Brick Hasfield says a key chain lets you lose all the keys at one time.

DREAMS WITH MR. SEARS

In the precious idle moments on Grandpa's farm, a Sears Roebuck and Co. catalogue provided nourishment for our daydreams. To wit . . .

A man's cashmere overshirt, 75 cents; pair of suspenders, 25 cents; pair of men's gloves, 58 cents; pocket knife, 40 cents; and a gallon of barn paint, 60 cents.

A bottle of Orange Wine Stomach Bitters, 75 cents; bottle of Little Liver Pills, $1.29; a railroad watch with 17 jewels, $20.50.

Pair of kangaroo shoes for men, $2.50; boy's felts and overs, $1.30; ladies' high button beaver felt shoes, $1.50; man's flannel shirt, $1; a derby hat, $1.49.

A lady's union suit, 89 cents; Remington double barrel 12-gauge shotgun, $10; a Spaulding baseball, $1.25; a man's suit, with vest, $13.50; lady's 20-inch hair switch, 90 cents; a man's toupee, $5.50 and a lady's plush cape, $9:35.

All this from a 1900 catalogue, when $8 a week was good pay. Our memory was jogged upon seeing this catalogue, belonging to Ned and Mildred Stanton of Verona.

★   ★   ★

From Grandpa's library of knowledge through humor:

An Indian chief summoned his three sons, told them the tribe was in dire need of food which they were to obtain and bring home. Broken Arrow went to the west, Running Deer to the east and Falling Rock disappeared along the trail over the hill.

After the rainy season, Broken Arrow appeared with venison, Running Deer came back with a supply of corn. But Falling Rock never returned.

And that is why to this day you see signs along the road, saying: "Watch for Falling Rock!"

WAITING FOR SPRING

We may have inherited a "hanging-on winter" complex from our grandfather on Potato Hill. Anyone who likes to get his hands in the soil knows the urge to get started in the garden, the deep desire for steady bombardments of sunlight so that seed may be sown, even if only the lowly lettuce.

Grandpa put in "waitin'-time" at odd jobs, like sharpening scythes, not a favorite pastime of a young grandson called upon to turn the grindstone.

There was a horse-drawn mowing machine which accomplished most of the hay cutting, but Grandpa was a thrifty fellow who insisted upon hand cutting in the corners and along the fences so that he could harvest all the crop. When he and Grandma established their small farm, he would cut his hay with a scythe, a long tedious job.

Scythes were one of the tools that could be prepared for the season in days when the frost was leaving the ground, before the fields were ready for soil preparation. A young grandson was useful, almost a necessity, for the grindstone had to be turned, for hours and hours, or so it seemed to the operator of the crank handle.

Water dripped from a hole in the bottom of a tin can suspended over the circular round stone. The blade sharpened better in a damp situation. Finally, after repeated testings with a thumb along the sharp edge and numerous tune-ups in doubtful spots, the scythe was ready for action.

Now time to look for woodchuck holes? Not yet. Grandpa simply took up another, sometimes larger scythe or a hand sickle and the process began again. When he finally hung up his cutting tools by their leather thong or snath in their proper places in his shop, a grandson was ready to test the hedgerows for animal signs, his wisdom broadened by the old man's praise: "Good work, boy. Now you know, with play comes work, if you want to eat."

A lady asked about the patch we wear on our jacket. "It's The Company of Military Historians," we explained. "I believe in letting bybones by bygones," she said, as she walked away.

GRANDMA'S PARLOR

We pretty much had the run of the farmhouse on Potato Hill from back woodshed to the spare room off the kitchen. But that liberty did not include our grandparents' downstairs bedroom and that big, mysterious corner room off the living quarters—The Parlor!

No one went into that wonderful center of precious family hand-me-downs except for weddings and funerals. Our parents were married there; our Grandpa and an uncle were buried from there. (The above is unfair to Grandma. She dusted that shrine once a week.)

It was not a morbid place, that room with the big horsehair sofa, the colorful round rag rug, the marble top table loaded with knicknacks. Hand-knit doilies were part of every chair, even the maple rocker over in a corner. The family Bible, with all the records, had a prominent place.

Ancestral pictures lined the walls; family albums were bound in fancy trimmings. Some of the pictures were tintypes from the middle of the past century. We remember best the big glass balls filled with swirling currents of color and the large white and blue shells—"hold it to your ear and hear the ocean waves." Particularly, the ashtray Grandma had made of an oblong glass receptacle backed with cigar bands held in place by green felt glued to the glass.

Our paternal grandmother concentrated on cut and colored glass of various shapes and sizes and on albums filled with postcards of the many places she would never visit. Not to be forgotten was a stereoscope resting on one of her marble tables. We were never permitted to use it alone. But that didn't matter, our Potato Hill grandmother would take us on her lap and explain what we were seeing in the 3-D versions of her day.

★   ★   ★

SUNDAY NIGHT MEALS

Most families have favorite Sunday evening meals. Like Grandma's fried mush topped with an egg. (Our Lady still doesn't believe it.) Or Aunt Blanche's baked beans, as certain on a Saturday, and often Sunday night, as life and death.

Our Mother produced a dish she called upon when there was a

scarcity of more luxurious fare. Salt pork and milk gravy, splashed over baked potatoes. Doesn't sound like much and could be monotonous, but it would get one by until fortunes improved.

We married into a family where you could go hungry every Sunday evening unless you liked popcorn and milk. That isn't exactly the truth, not in our case. Our mother-in-law, a thoughtful, caring person, decided that if we did not relish popcorn and milk we could survive until Monday morning with two poached eggs on toast.

Which brings us back to Grandma's fried mush. The egg was not poached. That was too city-like. All eggs were made to be fried, she declared.

And those baked beans! Our aunt was the champion of the Hill in combining pea beans, salt pork, brown sugar and maple syrup. She would have given Grandma Brown a run for the money.

Brick Hasfield says if wives really dressed to please their husbands, they'd dress a lot faster.

GRANDPA WOULD LIKE THIS

If Grandpa had come across this in print he would have passed it from hand to hand among the folks of the neighborhood:

"A young couple about to be married were looking for a home in the country. Satisfying themselves that they had found a suitable one, they left. During the return journey the young lady was thoughtful and when asked the reason for her silence, she said: "Did you see a 'WC'?" meaning a water closet. Not being certain, the young man wrote the landlord inquiring where the WC was situated. The landlord did not understand what the initials meant but came to the conclusion, after thought, that the couple was inquiring about the Western Church.

He replied:

"I regret very much the delay in replying to your letter; but have the pleasure of telling you that the WC is situated nine miles from the house and is capable of seating 250 people. This is unfortunate for you if you are in the habit of going regularly, but you will be glad to know that a great many people take their lunch with them and make a day of it. Others that cannot spare the time go by auto, arriving just in time, but generally cannot wait. The last time my wife and I went was six years ago and we had to stand up. It may interest you to know that a bazaar is to be given to furnish the WC with plush seats as the members feel it is a long felt want. I may mention the fact it pains us not to go more often."

Brick Hasfield says the more unsuitable the TV program, the quieter the children.

BELIEVE IN GHOSTS?

We don't believe in ghosts, but we were exposed to them when we were young.

When Grandma went on ahead, 17 years after her Potato Hill mate, she rested in her coffin in the parlor of her daughter, our mother. When the family arose in the morning of the funeral, the top of the casket was loose and a comb was missing from her hair.

Ghosts in the parlor? If so it was our brother and our sister who confessed, years later, that they snuck downstairs, removed the lid of the casket—to see if Grandma was comfortable in her favorite house slippers! They never explained the missing comb.

Grandpa died in 1917, with the family at his bedside. We saw Grandma place silver dollars on his eyelids, "to keep his eyes closed." The morning of the funeral they, too, were gone. Grandma said, "Never ask about spirits."

And, not related to the family, we know of a Civil War buff who insists that his camera always fails to work when he seeks to photograph the stone breastworks between two big rocks on Devil's Den at Gettysburg. Because there is a picture of the body of a young

Confederate displayed there, dead behind the stone wall? Or is his ghost protesting the removal of that body from 50 yards away so that a photographer could take a more interesting picture?

OUR GRANDPARENTS

You write a lot about your Potato Hill grandfather; how about your grandmother and your other grandparents?

We have not intentionally ignored them; no one could be around that little, austere, hard-working English-background woman and not come under her influence. We did not see as much of our paternal grandparents. They lived miles away.

Our maternal Grandpa was a jolly old man, built close to the ground, weight around 190 pounds. He laughed a lot, forgave a young grandson his misadventures and gave generously of his time.

Grandma was stern, to a point, but always caring, like warming a bed in an ice-cold upstairs for a grandson and baking cookies to supplement the plentiful plain-fare food of day to day. She expected to be obeyed—and was.

Both were up in the morning at the same time, around 5:30. He was out of bed several times during the night, to attend to personal matters and, in the winter, to keep the living room stove going.

There was no overnight heat in the kitchen. While the old man —he was in his 70's in our days together—went to the barn for the morning chores, she started the fire in the kitchen range, drew water from the indoor pump if the line was not clogged with ice, put the part-frozen pancake batter on the front of the range and began breakfast. If the kitchen pump was frozen, she might draw water with the chain buckets from the outside well, a mean job on a frosty morning. This seldom happened because Grandma kept an emergency supply of water in two copper teakettles and the reservoir on the stove was supposed to be filled.

We did not have much time in our boyhood with our paternal grandparents, over in the hamlet with the grandiose name—Perry City.

But every night we were there was a joy—if it rained. We were always tucked into bed, under sloping ceiling in the upper hall bedroom, fitted with a single bed. With a gate across the stairway which came into the upper floor through this small space, it was more like a passageway than a room.

When it rained, persistent drops on the tin roof made dream music. Rain on the roof, a wonderful lullaby beckoning a young boy to faraway adventures.

Our paternal grandfather believed a man should start the day right and that meant fried potatoes, eggs and ham or bacon for breakfast, concluded with a wedge of pie. There was pie to end every breakfast we can remember in their house. How fortunate to be raised with grandparents, on both sides, who did not have much but who never stinted when it came to food. The Lady of Our House says that experience is our present trouble at the table.

Our Perry City folks were as kind as those of Potato Hill. Our paternal grandfather had been a 17-year-old guard at Elmira prison camp for Confederates. He told us stories of futile escape attempts by tunneling—only 17 prisoners were successful—but never spoke of the many deaths at Elmira. Andersonville, in Georgia, has been given much attention as a Civil War "hell hole" and properly so but Elmira was almost as bad in a severe northern winter. Among the 12,122 prisoners, there were 2,917 deaths there in a year and a half.

Perhaps what Grandfather saw of hungry rebels as a prison guard was a reason for his need for hearty breakfasts.

PART II

Boyhood Days on the Family Farm

Boyhood Days on the Family Farm

NO SCHOOL BUS DAYS

A young farm boy, in our time, did not worry about getting up on time to catch the school bus. There was no school bus and, more direct, his father made certain the boy was up to help with morning chores.

In the winter, this farm lad undressed down to his long underwear in the sitting room, piling his clothes on a chair, before going up to a cold bed under the eaves off the upstairs hall. In the morning, he made a dash down the stairs, still in his long underwear, which came off only for the Saturday night bath, to get into work clothes, standing as close as one could to the chunk stove his father had restocked before leaving for the barn.

The schedule, as we recall, was Dad up at 5, calls son, boy up and out by 5:20, morning chores (4 to 6 cows hand milked) by 6:45 and then breakfast, a change into school garb and off for the village school, five miles away.

Chores on a farm never end, morning and night, seven days a week. Those in pre-dawn hours on Dad's farm included pitching hay from the overhead mow sufficient for morning and night feedings of the horses, shoveling ensilage from the silo and into feeding troughs for the cows in the milk shed and milking one's share of the herd.

Once the milk was in the house, across the road from the barns, there was a handle to turn on a device that separated cream from

63

milk. It was not difficult, especially when one could smell the ham and eggs Mother was processing on the kitchen stove a few feet away.

Once breakfast was over and clothes that did not smell of cows substituted for the work outfit, it was time to think of school. That meant harnessing the road horse and, according to season, hitching it to a cutter or light buggy—a farm boy's school bus in those days. The horse was stabled in rented space in the village before the boy walked around the corner to school—to eye his favorite girl at a nearby desk and to study and recite, in that order.

Farm chores were waiting on his return from school—the same cycle, feeding stock, cleaning stables and cow barn, milking by hand.

(To avoid confusion, our educational pursuit involved walking a short distance, a mile or so, to our first district school; then from Dad's farm driving a horse and, finally, when we had exhausted all local educational resources, boarding in a preparatory school for the last two years of high school courses and from there to college for a year, at which point our family had run out of money, we had run out of educational attainments and the college ran us out. It was satisfying to be asked, years later, to counsel students at that institution as to career opportunities.)

Brick Hasfield says we need a human transmission that will shift the blame.

A DANCE TO REMEMBER

All of us have our "worst storm." Ours happened in the days of our young teens, when Mother and Dad were trying to make a living on a 100-acre farm about two miles across a small valley and up from the place where our grandparents once lived. This was after our young life with them.

There wasn't much to do in winter, socially, in those days. The road to the village, four miles off the hill, often was plugged with snowdrifts. There was no radio or television. The only links with the outside world were the party line phone and the RFD mailman, when he could get through. He was more dependable than the telephone system, which often was out of kilter.

It came our family's turn to host the neighborhood square dance. So the downstairs furniture was stored in the woodshed and in room corners. Dad borrowed chairs, bought ample food and fixed temporary stalls in barn and shed for visiting horses. Using old fence rail, this was not complicated.

A two-man band was hired. One man played an accordion and called sets, the other would manipulate the small organ that once belonged to Grandma.

Twenty or more folks, big and little, came in cutters and bobsleds. It was mid-January and the roads were open, with good sleighing, the crusted fields glistening in the moonlight.

All had arrived when the band leader called. It was snowing hard in the village and he wasn't about to risk a trip up past Potato Hill. Then it began to snow at our place, never to let up until the next morning when more than two feet of new stuff was on the ground.

What do you do at a farmhouse dance with no music and no caller? You did what you could—Mother played simple tunes on the organ and an old man called sets as best as he could remember. That calls and music often did not match made no matter.

All evening Mother offered coffee, lemonade and chocolate milk while Dad entertained male guests with frequent trips to hard cider barrels in the cellar.

Around midnight, Mother served escalloped oysters, not expensive in those days, accompanied by slices of baked ham, squash, homemade bread, coffee or milk and dark red chocolate cake and pumpkin pie. There were other dishes, like escalloped potatoes and baked beans that the neighbors brought.

It was apparent that no one was going to try to return home that night in a blizzard. So Dad and the other men made the horses as comfortable as possible, the younger kids were sent upstairs to bed and the dance went on, dissolving gradually into small groups snoozing in chairs around the walls of the three downstairs rooms.

The only outside passageway kept open led to the privy behind the woodshed.

By mid-morning, the blizzard had died out. The women produced breakfast, ham and eggs, and the men helped milk Dad's cows. Then they split into groups to break the roads with two bobsled teams to reach other farms to relieve the cows.

By noon, they were back in our house and Mother and the women had another meal ready. By nightfall, all the guests had departed, to fight their way back through drifts to their places.

That's enough to remember, nearly 70 years later, but there was something else—personal to a young boy in whom the sap was just beginning to run. There was a girl in the neighborhood, pretty and older, who once had smiled at us in school. We were seriously affected.

She was at the dance and there was plenty of time for us to be together, in some out-of-the-way place. But she never spoke to us, not once; she had her eye on a bigger kid and didn't even look our way.

We recall that snowbound square dance because we learned there that women can be fickle.

★ ★ ★

Brick Hasfield says no matter what a hospital charges for a private room you only get a semi-private gown.

MOTHER AT THE ORGAN

Our Mother was an untaught musician. She did not have a piano but she could play unforgettable tunes on a small parlor organ (old mail order catalogues say it cost between $30 and $40), pumping with side motions of her right knee.

Who recalls the comic song, "The Preacher and the Bear"? The minister out on a stroll through the woods is treed by a bear and his prayer, in song, is eloquent: "Oh, Lord, if you can't help me, please don't help that bear."

A sad song was from Civil War days, "Just Before the Battle, Mother" and even more melancholy (it made us cry), "I'm Tying the Leaves So They Won't Come Down," the attempt of a young boy to save his mother, having been told she would die "when the leaves come down."

Mother also played hymns, particularly "Rock of Ages" and "Abide With Me." They were sung at her funeral.

BEWARE JERSEY LIGHTNING

Without radio or television and with a limited supply of magazines, hard cider sipping was one way for long-ago countryside males to pass an evening before the living room stove, the wind blowing around the house corners and snow piling in the path to the barn. It could be more effective than a sleeping pill, given sufficient time to enjoy.

Applejack was something else. During Prohibition time it was called Jersey Lightning.

Mother would not permit the stuff in her house. But that didn't stop the manufacture of a limited amount in the barn, given sufficient cold weather.

Applejack was merely that part of hard cider in which the alcoholic content was so high as to resist any freeze. Hard cider was poured into a keg and left unprotected in below-zero weather until the cider froze—that is, became ice on the outer edges of the contents, the center concentrated alcohol, unfreezable liquid dynamite.

The core never froze—that was the applejack. It was drawn off by drilling into the frozen keg and transferring the applejack to bottles.

It was not that cold when it hit one's stomach; that drink, for tough men only, would quickly transfer one to warmer climates. We have one-time-only experience with applejack. We knew where our Father hid it and acquired limited first-hand knowledge of its potency. Never again!

THOSE FAITHFUL HORSES

The naming of race horses is an art, like writing headlines demanding graphic description in limited space. We do not know how the horses on the two farms of our memory came by their names.

Grandpa had two work horses, a young roader and two mules. The gelding our uncle hitched to his rubber-tired '"courting" carriage answered to Rock. The work team is lost in history, but the mules were Jack and Jim. Grandma said these were the names of two of the cavalry horses Grandpa rode in battle when he single-handedly saved the Union.

Our father had three horses, a traditional work team and a colt of near adult age named Prince. He was too skittish for our use. That was well with us; when we took a girl to a dance in the village, to a church supper or an ice cream festival, we drove King, a big, plodding bay, dependable but slow and not very bright.

King was the kind that, when walking home after a long night, his youthful driver asleep on the buggy seat, was apt to drift off into a field of standing corn, rig and all, for a midnight snack. But he would eventually get us home, standing faithfully in the night before the horse barn door until we awoke.

His companion in team traces was Molly, a quiet black mare who knew how to keep King pulling his share and who never had to be guided by a sharp human tongue. Farm boys, in our days, learned to swear trying to steer a cantankerous team hitched to a plow on a rocky side hill.

Once, when King tripped and fell over his own feet while hitched to the hay wagon, Molly stood quietly by as we got the downed horse out of his harness. Grandpa had told us that the worst problem with kicking and threshing wounded horses in the war was "cutting" them out of artillery teams, survivors rearing and plunging, shells bursting nearby.

We also had a Shetland pony and a cart. Babe belonged to us, Dad said, but we were getting too old for belt-high ponies and Babe became the possession of our sister and much younger brother.

Molly pulled the one-horse hay rake and turned around by herself at the end of the pull on the horsefork. Kind and gentle, she liked to have people in her stall. She would whinny when we opened the stable door and she was the one who got an extra allotment of blackstrap molasses when it came time to distribute that delicacy from the big open-ended barrel.

She was the oldest. One morning we went to the barn to do the chores and found Molly dead in her stall. We cried.

It is almost impossible to believe today, but in that Great Depression of the 1930's a seventh of all the people able to work in this nation were idle, five million families were supported by charity. There was no unemployment insurance, no welfare as we know it now, no Social Security or any of the agencies of assistance as we now have today. Welfare often was a bushel of potatoes, a sack of coal and a few dollars.

BOY BEHIND A PLOW

We are told that the first patent for a cast iron plow was issued in 1770. Before that, so long ago as to be unrecorded, man turned the soil with wooden blades. Even before then, he scratched the dirt with a stick, anything to make a thin layer of humus hospitable to seed.

Now powerful machines pull many plows, in an angled row, turning over more sod in a single pass than horse-pulled rigs of long ago could accomplish in an hour.

In our time on Father's farm, in a five-acre field, we were day after day gripping the handles of a one-blade steel plow, pulled by a team of horses, old King plodding in the furrow, Molly alongside.

Anyone who has spent time with such a device will have thicker skin on the back of his left shoulder where the reins passed around his neck and under his right arm. He will also recall, clearly, those times of sudden crisis when the plow tip hit an imbedded rock and the plow handles flew up out of control while he was desperately trying to halt the team. Men and boys have been hurt seriously while walking, sometimes in a dream, behind a plow on a rocky, hillside farm.

Men took pride in the precise cut of their plow, particularly in new ground. Those who plowed straight furrows earned the respect of their neighbors.

Brick Hasfield says many a husband wishes he had as much fun when he is out as his wife thinks he does.

CIDER PRESSING TIME

In olden days, most farms had a hand-powered cider mill. Men of authority and girth, now sitting behind city desks, can recall.

Thrifty farmers used the windfall apples and "sortings" to put down a few barrels of sweet cider, some for immediate beverage use, some for vinegar and, for many so inclined, a reserve of golden liquid requiring time to gain potency. Hard cider is well known in history, the chief beverage for the men in the ranks who fought to establish this nation.

Making cider with a hand press is not fun, as old farm boys will testify. The apples were ground in the wooden hopper, the juicy mess then placed in the tub, the screw pressing the wooden cover against the mass, the sweet juice dripping into an open half hogshead.

The ingenuity of man has produced various fluid combinations, but none quite equals fresh-pressed apple juice. We know cider well, in several forms—sweet, hard and concentrated, the latter often called applejack, a blow-your-head-off domestic liquor.

The above was written before we had the opportunity to test our memories of old-time, hand-powered cider presses—high on a mountain near Boone, North Carolina, at the attractive, if unusual, home built by our grandson, Tom Philipp and his Kay. We had accompanied Our Lady, Tom's mother, Shirley Kudla, and her husband, Bill, to see the North Carolina family—Tom, Kay and two of our great-grandchildren, Amber Sunshine and Anna Kate.

Our description of the cider press of our youth checked when our grandson drove up his hill with a borrowed 1890ish cider mill, manufactured in Batavia, New York, and now owned by his "food co-op."

Built on four sturdy two-by-fours, the co-op press has the wooden hopper which feeds slicing-grinding blades in a round throat, the energy supplied by operating a crank on one side or, if the device plugs, by turning a large counter-balancing iron wheel on the opposite side, either of which provide the necessary power through a set of gears.

The sliced and mashed apples land in a slat-sided tub in which the drippy mess is pressed by a wood top and a big hand screw until all the juice has run into a wooden trough to drip into whatever is handy at the end of the process.

★　★　★

OLD-TIME FARMING

Threshing time was worth waiting for, not for the men, who labored hard when the big cumbersome machine came to the farm, but for a boy mystified by the working of a big, steam-powered apparatus which could move along a road and then, solidly in place, spin a big wheel to make its threshing machine work.

It was a mobile steam engine harnessed by a long, wide leather belt to a mysterious and noisy long box which took in wheat, oats, rye or buckwheat at one end, separated the grain from the stalks, and blew the straw out the back end into a barn mow or a stack in the field. The grain came pouring out a chute on one side, to be carried to a rodent-proof granary or sacked for sale.

Some attention, in a piece like this, should be given to harvesting field beans, the dry ones which produce the delicious, brown-sugar flavored baked beans, one of the best of foods.

Forking bean vines, pulled from the ground with dirt clinging to the roots, into small piles for drying and then pitching them onto wagons for the trip to the threshing machine was one of the dirtiest of farm jobs.

We may not have been a typical farm boy. We liked haying and threshing—as long as we were not ordered into a dusty, hot mow under a tin roof. Cultivating was monotonous, picking potatoes hard work, now called "stooped labor." We did not mind filling silo as long as we could drive the team as the men folks pitched bundles of corn on the hayrick. Tramping ensilage inside the big wooden tube kept one jumping to stay ahead of the imput.

Getting in the hay could be fun, when one reached an age to be trusted with a mower. In our experience, a boy's work in a hay field was usually atop a horse-drawn rake, activated by foot pressure on a pedal to dump the partly rolled-up hay into an irregular row, from which it would be forked into haycocks for seasoning before being hand pitched onto a wagon. If a hayloader was available, lacking on Grandpa's place but used at Dad's farm later, the boy's job was to drive the team, straddling the hay row, while what we then thought was an ingenious device carried the hay from the field onto the wagon.

Transferring potatoes, torn from their nest in the ground by a horse-drawn potato digger, into bushel crates, by hand, was plain, old-fashioned hard work. The crates, when filled, weighed 40 pounds or more. Luckily we were deemed too small for lifting; all we had to do was pick potatoes from the ground, put them into a burlap sack worn from a shoulder and dump them into the crates.

For all this, threshing is to be remembered, many years later, for the great meals, noon and night provided by the women of the family. Every one of them was in unspoken competition for praise from the threshers, particularly the crew that took the machine from farm to farm, and knew the best of the neighborhood cooks.

Perhaps more about "dinner for threshers" later. We are not sufficiently hungry at this moment.

Brick Hasfield says old age ain't for sissies.

DINNER FOR THRESHERS

The day the threshing machine, towed by a big steam engine, came could be one of disagreeable work for a boy assigned to a dusty straw mow but it also was the time of "dinner for threshers," a wonderful feast.

The neighborhood men swapped work, helping each other at labor-intensive jobs. The favor was returned, so that it might take four days of threshing to get one accomplished on your farm.

The wives also "swapped," collecting at the farm involved with tasty casseroles, breads and desserts. Mother would return the obligation when the time came to help out with dinner up or down the road.

"Dinner for threshers" was a meal of farm produced foods— pork, beef, veal or lamb, escalloped or mashed potatoes, home grown vegetables, eggs, breads and biscuits. And, of course, always baked beans, pies and cakes galore and big mugs of coffee.

The responsibility of a young boy, if released from threshing duty, was to take charge of the "wash up." He built a fire outside, by the side door, under a big iron kettle for steaming hot water. He had handy, on a long bench by the woodshed, sufficient wash basins, soap and towels, along with a supply of cold spring water to temper that from the fire. Our Mother insisted that a mirror be attached to the side of the house and plenty of combs provided for those wishing to "tidy up."

We never were privileged to eat with the men, but there always was sufficient food for the women and the boy after he had cleaned up the wash area.

"Dinner for threshers!" Even better than some church suppers and most of them are magnificent.

We were raised, for a while, in a small village where . . . if you missed church the get-well-cards began coming . . . you could get a wrong number and talk for 15 minutes . . . and folks would ask how you felt and actually listen to your answer.

ONE-ROOM SCHOOL DAYS

There has been uncovered in our family files, after being hidden for more than half a century, a postcard bearing the picture of the pupils and teacher of a rural district school.

The 20 pupils, ranging in age sufficient for study in all eight grades, are bright-eyed and in their best, the older girls with big bows on their hair, the older boys wearing wide neckties. The younger girls look the happiest, not knowing of life's cares, and the smaller boys are all classified by the wearing of galluses holding up what in more sophisticated circles would be called knickers, these over knee-length black stockings.

The young woman teacher of all eight grades, in a skirt that almost sweeps the ground, is smiling as if proud of her charges.

District school then was almost totally unlike elementary classes of today. There was no "head start," no kindergarten, no teacher's aides, no school buses, no special attention to "disturbed" children, no school lunches, no special examinations, no bans on spanking—and no pupil demonstrations.

We will contend that morale in that multi-grade school was high, with few problems. What there were were handled quickly and expertly by the teacher. Only infrequently did she refer mischief detrimental to the tranquility of the day to higher authorities. When she did, she marched home with the offending child to make a first-hand report to the parents. We affirm that this procedure was effective, for whatever punishment had been administered in school was enlarged upon at home.

We have noted the absence of school lunches, one of modern education's better programs, but each morning that teacher took a little boy and his equally small sister into the attached woodshed and gave them milk, a cookie or fried cake. She was providing a bit of breakfast to youngsters, from a poor family (not ours) who came to school without a morning meal.

This picture means much to us because it contains an average appearing third grader of no great promise—who now cannot recall the name of the teacher, but who does cherish her as the one who showed him the joy of reading.

★　★　★

THE OLD SWIMMING HOLE

If we could turn back the years and be a boy again, we'd head for the "ol' swimmin' hole." It's still there; we see it every time we go back, stopping if only for a moment to dream.

It is almost as it was then, a large circular pothole, 10 feet or more deep, 8 or 9 feet in diameter, cut into solid rock at the foot cf a miniature falls in a creek formed millions of years ago.

This is not a conventional swimming hole, a quiet spot of water in a placid stream, where one could actually swim. This is a bath-tub in the rocks, stingy-cold water streaming down a series of falls and swirling around this natural receptacle before continuing its steep downward flow to the lake hundreds of feet below. The stream is three to four inches deep around the hole, the smooth rock slippery.

The pothole is below and to one side of a highway bridge; we jumped into it nude then and they still plunge into it in the same fashion. It was an all-male preserve; if females intruded you simply sought shelter in the pool, shouting taunts and threats to come out, as you were, until the invaders went away. One brazen hussy actually stole our clothes, but that's another story. We used to think she would come to no good. She married a preacher!

You cannot see the hole from a vehicle on the bridge. Motorists thunder across the span today just as horses and wagons did then. It gave a feeling of bravado to be dunking in the raw while civilization passed, unknowing, overhead.

The water, in the eons that creek has been running, has made twisting slides of smooth, wet rock on which a bare-tailed boy could, and still can, slide for yards before plunging feet first, into the pool.

You didn't swim; you dunked. But you forgot the heat and you put out of mind the hot work which always waited in dry, dusty fields.

If you had ever dunked yourself in that pothole under the bridge, you could never find satisfaction in a man-made pool with static water.

★　★　★

LIFE WITH CULTIVATORS

Corn in Central New York is supposed to be "knee high by the Fourth of July." Production of this crop, this nation's greatest, has changed greatly since we rode a two-wheeled cultivator up and down corn rows, fighting weeds which often grew faster than the corn.

Now the land is dosed with poison to eliminate the weeds and the corn, which ignores it, does not have to share the energies of the soil with interlopers. That relegates cultivators, walking and riding, to the status of farm antiques.

We presume there are those who have no acquaintance with a walking cultivator. Dragged by one horse and steered by a boy gripping rear handles, it was a device armed with teeth and blades that stirred the soil and executed some of the weeds. Most all farm horses trained to harness knew enough not to step on the plants, be they corn, beans or potatoes, and the rig was not difficult to steer away from the rows on either side.

A team of two horses was required for operation of a two-wheeled riding cultivator, on which the operator rode in an uncomfortable steel seat, feet on steering rods and eyes on the row which passed beneath him, one wheel on each side.

It was not difficult work. It was easier than pitching hay into cocks or onto a wagon or mowing straw in a hot, dusty barn. But it was monotonous, up and down the rows, with never a change of scenery before one's eyes trained steadily on the passing plants, the imperative mission being to keep the corn, the potatoes or the beans undamaged.

A young boy could create a world of his own as he traveled the rows, back and forth, back and forth. A growing corn field, not yet at a height which made weeding impractical, was suited for dreaming, for visualizing in one's mind the day one would depart from the lonely hill for the wonders of the world over the horizon.

Cultivating certainly did no harm to the formation of a young, useful life. The farm boy we knew did not complain, as long as he had the assurance of a horse and buggy to go to a dance or a picture show in the town at the foot of the hill.

★   ★   ★

WE ATE IT ALL

Most every housewife knows how to make pumpkin pie. Of course, the degree of excellence will vary, as it does in any such relationship.

There are various kinds of pumpkin pie, as anyone who has been to a church supper can testify. There are the thin ones with lacy black tops. There are soft, fat wedges that melt in one's mouth. And all sorts in between.

We like all of them. But we must protest against drowning good pumpkin pie under a big blob of imitation whipped cream. That's no way to treat one of the finest American kitchen products.

Our knowledge of pumpkin pie dates back to young years, a memory of personal greed. Our mother baked a pumpkin pie and placed in on the window sill of an open window, accessible on both sides. Always hungry, then as now, we came by and ate all of it.

We suffered, inside and on the rear end.

Brick Hasfield says a bachelor is a fellow who can pull on his socks from either end.

TWO SHORTS AND A LONG

The first rural telephone system we knew did not have a phone book, merely a list of names and ring numbers on a piece of cardboard, posted on the wall. The central switchboard in the village, connecting the 15 or so subscribers on our party line with perhaps 200 or more telephones in the area, was signaled by buzzes—two shorts and a long.

These new walk-around phones of today are far relatives of the old oblong wooden box with two bells at the top and a black mouthpiece attached to a moveable long neck that could be adjusted to the height of one's mouth from the floor. You listened through a bell-shaped contrivance that hung on an up-and-down cradle on the left side of the box on the wall. It was on a cord and you held it to your ear while you talked into the black gizmo on the neck piece.

On the right of the phone box was a crank which, when turned, attracted the attention of the attendant in the central office or, according to the ring, summoned a neighbor on the party line.

To operate this contraption, you took the receiver off the hook and listened to learn if the line was "busy." (To the oldsters who remember, don't hang up on us . . . there are a lot of younger folks who don't even recall the Korean War, let alone a hand-cranked rural telephone system.)

If the line was in use and the conversation interesting, one might listen in. The rural party line was the community radio. All participants could "get" each other by ringing the proper code, but only those in the neighborhood pool.

If the line was clear, you hung up the receiver, wound the crank, took down the receiver and waited. Finally Miss Jones at Central would say "Operator" or some appropriate greeting. She never said, "Number, please?" You asked for parties by name, not number.

It was not difficult to set up a conference call, although that term was unknown. You could hear a series of clicks as receivers came off the hook and before long you could be talking to four or five neighbors and have only called one. If you wanted to leave two or three frustrated women burning with curiosity, all you had to say, when the line was full, was, "This is a hot one, I'll tell you when I see you."

If you were not going to be home, you might arrange with a neighbor to take your calls—two shorts and a long.

When our brother, Harold, was 14 or so, after we had gone on to matrimony, he became the night operator in the village telephone exchange. He learned how to sleep, bit by bit, along with buzz-buzz interruptions. He was the town's security watch, information post and all-around watchdog, even on the habits of the resident citizens. He knew where the doctor could be reached, where the fire was, who was ill, and when the church supper was scheduled. He also learned a lot of gossip.

The system was not difficult to maintain. All the subscribers had to do was to keep the line up on their property and have two workable dry batteries in the phone box. To a young boy, it was a mystery that worked.

Brick Hasfield says the difference between genius and stupidity is that genius has its limits.

DAYS OF DIME NOVELS

We were nine or ten when we discovered our first "dime novel." It may have been Frank Merriwell in "Diamond Land" or perhaps "His One Ambition," or "The Mishaps of a Boy Reporter."

More likely it was a Nick Carter, Buffalo Bill or Jesse James. We remember them better than stories such as "Pluck & Luck, from Bootblack to Senator" or "Pure Grit, a Climb from the Slums to Happiness and Progress."

We liked Fred Fearnot in the "Wild Beast" and a now forgotten young hero in "A Week at the Circus." It fact, we liked everything we could get to read, to this day a compulsion.

Mother did not object to what she called "good" books, but we had to hide our accounts of the Younger brothers, Cole, James, Robert and John, famous American desperadoes; Bowery Bill and, of course, Nick Carter, the great detective.

There are men who will remember their "secret places" where they hid from their mothers to enjoy forbidden tales of high adventure—hay lofts, attics, privies, even in the high corn.

We had a very limited supply of dimes, but our possession of such material was not limited by our cash resources. There were other boys of like age close at hand and we were part of a well regulated traveling library, circulation—underground.

Mother frowned sternly upon "trash," but we doubt that our life was changed by reading such tales. If they aroused us, it was not in the direction of present day "literature," but rather to be resolute, courageous, quick on the draw and a keeper of one's word.

THE ATTRACTION AT CHURCH

We went to the morning church services with Mother and, in the evening, alone, in response to our own motivation. Alone because at night we went to the other church.

There were—and are—two churches in the village, the Presbyterian near our house and the Methodist across the mill pond, up by the railroad depot. Sometimes we went to both on Sunday night, not attending the services, but hanging around outside for one specific purpose—to see "our girl" as she came from Epworth League or Christian Endeavor. That special one may not have realized she had that distinction; often, as we remember, we seemed not to have made much of an impression with certain young ladies.

Just to see the girl you liked, perhaps even to be permitted to walk her home, not even holding her hand, was the reward for waiting outside the church. Why didn't we go inside, why did we not attend services as good boys should have done? Mother thought we did. Perhaps it was the influence of bigger boys who spurned such faithfulness and enforced their presence upon younger ones of that informal group—not a gang—that hung around together, around the churches on Sunday nights.

The village doctor was so busy giving injections at the peak of the cold virus season that those who gathered at the barber shop tacked a sign at his office door: "To Save Time Please Back Into Office."

OLD TIME MEALS

There comes a time, just before the arrival of Spring, when our favorite cook will ask: "How would you like parsnip stew tonight?" This is one of her many attributes, hinting that solid old-fashioned foods might be good for us.

If parsnip stew stirs curiosity, it is a splendid dish of lamb, pork, potatoes and parsnips. Because the greater part of the population has no liking for parsnips many do not know this delicious Spring tonic. Once upon a time we would pity the pigs if we had to feed them parsnips.

We probably would stir limited support among the young in our population if we campaigned for tasty dishes of long ago—chipped beef on baked potatoes, cod fish gravy, popcorn and milk, pork and beans baked with brown sugar, fried corn mush, fresh peas and new potatoes in light cream, and of course, salt pork and gravy.

We are not in favor of eliminating slick pictured meal packages that bring emancipation from hours in the kitchen. But we have no relish for food subdued to submission under steam pressure, pills that turn water into soup and some of the ready-to-eat nourishments that line grocery shelves.

When we were growing up with grandparents on Potato Hill, salt pork with creamy, white gravy was a staple. The farm-produced salt pork, laced with strips of lean meat, was fried until crisp and chewey. Undercooked salt pork can still spoil an evening.

The gravy was rich, thick and decorated with rivulets of melted butter. Never margarine, Grandma churned her own butter.

Brick Hasfield says a brat is a child who acts like your own, but belongs to a neighbor.

HARVESTING ICE

The village pond, fed by a sizable creek, was closely watched as the weather grew colder. Once ice was formed thick enough to bear the weight of a man, the surface was kept clear of snow and daily tests of thickness conducted.

When the ice was at least nine inches—12 to 14 were more desirable—farmers and village residents with ice houses gathered with their tools, the pond being big enough to handle the demand if "cut over" a couple of times.

Cutting ice meant spudding holes through the frozen surface so that a long hand-powered saw could work its way to make a wide opening over the water. Then the cutters would go to work sawing lanes to the nearby shores where the ice cakes, of various sizes, could be pushed to the bank for loading onto sleds by horsepower. Transported to ice houses, the cakes were laid in orderly fashion, side by side, protected by clean sawdust. Ice stored properly in this fashion would last through the hottest summer.

Those were days without automatic refrigeration powered by electricity. Even with a supply of ice handy, Mother preferred the coolness of the cellar, with its hard-trod dirt floor. The smell there is difficult to describe, but lingers in memory.

Life without automatic refrigeration seems impossible today, but there are men and women who remember how they did without and easily because they did not know any other way.

A word to the wise: Beware of your wife calling you a model husband. Model can mean "a small imitation of the real thing."

A TASTE OF BRIMSTONE

Everyone raised on a hilly farm has had experiences with lightning. Farmers live with the weather and big storms are expected. The unpredictable danger of lightning is always present.

While working in a hay field, an uncle suddenly said, "Come on, we are going in." The field was close to the farm house and we made it to the stoop without getting wet.

As we stood on the porch, watching black clouds coming over the back hills, a bolt of lightning struck a herd of cows in a pasture across the road, no more than 150 yards from the house. Both uncle and boy were stunned, the air filled with brimstone.

The uncle dashed into the kitchen, grabbed a butcher knife and ran to the cows, several lying motionless on the ground. They belonged to a neighbor, but nevertheless our uncle cut the throats of three dead cows so that the meat would be useable.

Years later, when we were trying to help our father on a hillside farm a couple miles up from the homestead, a storm approached and he backed a load of hay into the barn, holding the horses by their bridles until the rain stopped. We were on top of the hay load.

Suddenly a bolt hit a lightning rod on the barn and the electric charge followed the ground wires to the earth, passing a few feet from the barn door and the team. Both horses and Dad were knocked down, we were thrown off the load to the barn floor and all four were senseless for a time. When we recovered we again tasted brimstone for hours.

While in college, we were participating in football practice and a group of trackmen were 100 yards away at the end of the field. Thunder was grumbling on the horizon.

Without warning, lightning hit one of the trackmen, killing him instantly, and knocking others in the group around like tenpins hit by a ball.

We do not like lightning.

Things we did not know as a child . . .

That the brassiere was invented in 1912 by an American "for a painfully endowed young opera singer." That Kleenex was first used as a World War I gas mask filter. That pretzels originated with French monks in 610 A.D. and that Jewish matzos became the first pizza, thousands of years ago, when Roman soldiers smeared them with olive oil and cheese.

MOTHER'S GREAT MOMENT

We were brought up on eye-witness accounts of the shooting of a President of the United States. Our mother saw William McKinley mortally wounded by an assassin at the Buffalo Pan-American

Exposition of 1901.

She was yet to be married, a young country district school teacher who, with another young woman, dreamed for months about their trip on the Lehigh Valley Railroad from the Village of Burdett, New York, to Buffalo. The man who was to be our father four years later had just proposed; this was to be her last single fling.

After spending the night with a relative, they were at the Exposition Ground early September 6, 1901 to have a place in line in the Temple of Music so that they could shake the hand of the President.

While waiting about two hours (the time span grew longer as Mother advanced in age) she and her friend noticed a slight-built, dark individual four places ahead of them. He did not speak; his right hand was wrapped in a handkerchief.

President McKinley arrived and, standing almost alone, without protection, began to greet the people. Mother said, "It was a nice scene, the President amid all the pretty flowers." Born into an agricultural Democratic family far different from today's urban Democrats, she was about to shake the hand of the Republican president who had a good record in his first term, including the winning of the Spanish-American War, and was then eight months into his second.

Mother's account of what happened was generally consistent over the years. The young man with the wrapped hand approached the President, extended his left hand and simultaneously fired two bullets into the President's body from a weapon concealed by the handkerchief.

Mother recalled, "We heard two noises and Mr. McKinley say, rather loudly, 'Am I shot?' Some men were wrestling with the young man, both of us were pushed off our feet into tall potted plants. I tore my new dress."

For the rest of her long life, she told the same story. How someone helped her and her companion to their feet, how the assailant was hustled away, shouting something, face bloody, and how the President was carried away, clutching his abdomen. She and her friend were taken aside and questioned by two strange men. They were not called as witnesses at the trial.

They left the Temple of Music and did not, Mother said, enjoy the rest of the day and on the next returned by train to Schuyler County—with much to tell for the rest of her life.

President McKinley appeared to be recovering when his condition worsened and he died September 14, 1901. Theodore Roosevelt became president.

The 28-year-old killer, Leon F. Czolgosz (Chol-gosh) was judged sane and electrocuted before the year end, declaring McKinley was an enemy of the working people. The press of that day said he was an anarchist.

When Mother was in her 80's, she insisted what had happened before her eyes in Buffalo was not so unusual, with all the bad things she had been reading about in the many years since then.

Brick Hasfield says a perfect example of minority rule is having a baby in the house.

DECORATION DAY

We are committed to a single Memorial Day—not one traditional and one "observed," almost a week apart. Our devotion to this special observance goes back to childhood days when Decoration Day, as it was then called, was the occasion for the annual visit to the cemetery.

It remains Decoration Day to those who can recall talking to the old men who fought in the great Civil War which gave birth to the national observance of memory and appreciation.

Decoration Day fitted the life of a small community. Veterans' auxiliaries—the Sons and Daughters of those honored—provided color bearers and guards; the school band played; children marched carrying little flags. A bugler played taps in the cemetery; church groups served lunch. Many of the survivors of the war never heard that bugle call in their time of service, it being written in mid-war days by General Daniel Butterfield of Utica and not universally used until after the hostilities.

A dwindling small group of veterans walked proudly in the parade as long as they could; then they rode in the automobiles of those days—antiques now—when they could march no more. They never seemed able to transmit the drama of their days gone by. They seldom smiled; they spoke sparingly; they appreciated the dignity of the day. Even in our childhood, we were convinced that all wars were fought by old men.

After the formalities, young boys remained in the cemetery, reading names cut into stone, playing "war" with wooden guns from behind the grave shafts—youthful dreams vivid, almost real. Decoration Day!

Brick Hasfield says don't treat your body as if you had a spare in the trunk.

THE RAILROAD STATION

The railroad depot was one of the "hang-outs" of the young boys in the village. It was a fairly large wooden structure, beside the two-track Lehigh Valley main line, windows grimy and gray clapboards stained with years of soot. It still stands, converted to a distribution center for agricultural needs.

The gray exterior blended with a dirt-stained narrow board floor. The inner walls were lined with curved seat benches, originally brightly varnished. A large pot-bellied, cast-iron stove stood in the center, resting on bricks in a square, open box filled with sand. The metal stovepipe made several turns to the chimney in the wall.

At the north side was the agent's office, a small area behind a grilled ticket window, its wide front windows jutting beyond the line of the building. The agent-telegrapher could see up and down the tracks as far as the big curves, a mile or so in each direction.

From there came the clatter of the telegraph, speaking a language all youngsters wished they would learn. This fascinating sound thrilled those who knew it was a direct connection with the outside world they dreamed about. Posters of wanted men, sought for crimes against the railroad, offered the standard $500 reward. Young boys could ponder how they would use that princely sum once they had caught the desperadoes.

Beyond the office was the baggage room, from which a steel-wheeled high platform cart carried baggage and small freight to the trains' baggage cars. Usually the load of the station baggageman—the agent with a different hat—was composed of travelers' trunks and farmers' cream cans and egg crates.

The passenger trains, two locals each way each day, plus two non-stopping "Limiteds," connecting Jersey City with Buffalo, have long disappeared. So have the long freight trains, driven into oblivion by highway trucks. The once prosperous Lehigh Valley, a model operation for its size in the early 1900s, has vanished, its only marks now the old depots along the abandoned right-of-way where trees now impede snowmobile travel.

A child, turned old man, can return to the deserted depot, ignore its present commercial uses, and stand on the old platform. He can close his eyes and hear the evening local, bell clanging and steam hissing, come down the rails, stopping for brief minutes and then . . . "all aboard, all aboard . . ." followed by the unforgotten sounds of the train disappearing around the bend in the distance, headed for the big city. We all need to go back and listen.

Brick Hasfield says a second-story fellow is a man whose wife doesn't believe the first.

OUR FIRST AIRPLANE

It was a hot summer afternoon. We were dozing in the seat of a two-wheeled cultivator, the team plodding along between rows of bean vines. Suddenly, something we had never seen before came flying low over the woodlot, headed on a right-angled course before our stunned eyes.

There, in that field on Dad's farm, in 1920, we saw our first airplane. It was a big wood and wire affair with what looked like big canoes on each side. A hydroplane we learned.

Glenn Curtiss, experimenting with off-water planes at Hammondsport on Lake Keuka, had flown over to Seneca Lake for demonstrations, we read later in the weekly paper. We declare, to this day, that a man wearing goggles waved to an astonished boy from that airplane, the sudden sight of which nearly lifted that boy in amazement from that cultivator seat.

Brick Hasfield says walking the floor with the baby is good practice for later on when that baby is out all night with the family car.

HORNING BEE TUNE

SHIVAREE: A noisy serenade to a newly married couple expected to provide refreshments to silence the serenaders—Webster. On Potato Hill, they called it a "Horning Bee."

A bachelor down the road a piece finally married a widow he had been escorting to Grange meetings and church suppers. A man of sufficient means, he took his bride to Niagara Falls, returning secretly, they hoped, after four or five days on their honeymoon.

Within a week of their return, the more friendly and adventuresome on the Hill paid their respects to the couple. We tagged along, even if it was long past bedtime.

There were 20 or more outside the home of the newlyweds around 10 that night, equipped with all types of noisemakers, horns, tin pans, whistles, anything, on signal, to make a commotion. Excellent for the purpose was a big circular saw blade, carried on a crowbar and banged with the back side of an axe.

The couple finally made an appearance and "faced the music," serving cider, coffee, fried cakes, cookies, some of which had been thoughtfully brought along by female serenaders.

Finally, the neighbors cleared out, or pretended to, and the couple returned to their marriage bed to find that someone had sneaked into their bedroom amid the jollities and attached cowbells to the underside of the bed springs.

In 1845, Congress passed a law setting the first Tuesday after the first Monday in November as the presidential election nationwide. November was selected because, it is said, harvesting was over and the roads were not yet impassable. As a result, Election Day never falls on the first of November or later than the eighth.

★　★　★

TALES OF THREE SKUNKS

Mustelidae has a muscular walled perineal gland from which it can eject, when in danger or scared, an intensely malodorous secretion. That's what the reference book says.

Farm boys, in our time and now, were well educated about skunks, but not in those terms. That the skunk had a near perfect defense long before chemical warfare was well known.

Skunks were to be avoided, but a young fellow with sufficient know-how could run a trap line and, if sufficiently lucky, secure a half-stripe and perhaps obtain a dollar and a half from the fur dealer. It was smelly, unattractive work, but a dollar was a dollar.

Many have true stories about skunks, ranging from the faint odors that persist along high-speed highways to disasterous encounters.

First, the unusual that became family lore. In dark hours, Mother heard a faint noise at the windowsill and went over, asking, "Kitty, Kitty, you want to go out?" Suddenly, she realized she was talking to a skunk, gazing out of the second story bedroom window. A skunk in the house!

She fled the room, leaving an alarmed father asking what was going on. (He always denied that he stood upright in the bed and swore. Mother said you could see his footprints deep in the mattress.)

How to get a live skunk out of an upstairs room without having to evacuate the house?

Downstairs the family held a fruitless council. Then our little sister, about seven, came downstairs and announced the skunk "was gone." A cautious investigation proved she was wrong. The skunk had retreated into a dark corner of a long, walk-in closet.

Dad's luck held. There was an empty trunk in the closet. He carefully turned it on its side and opened the lid several inches. Everyone waited, several hours. Later, a close look showed no skunk in sight; it was in the trunk. He closed the lid and persuaded his young son to help carry the box, skunk and all, down the stairs and out of the house.

The trunk, taken down the road some distance, was placed in the same position as in the closet, on its side, lid partly open on the ground. "Watch out," Dad ordered, as we retreated.

Suddenly, our foolhardy sister ran up as a mystified young skunk started to emerge from the trunk. Ignoring parental screams, she leaned over the trunk, grabbed the skunk by the tail and quickly hoisted it high in the air, harmless with rear feet off the ground.

The family was petrified. She laughed and began to chase her brother, skunk in hand. We fled. Finally, she tossed the skunk over a stonewall and dashed away. The dazed skunk walked off, dignity shaken, reservoir of protection full. After a while, Dad laughed and forgot about a talk with Sister.

Our other skunk highlight was different, a disaster which cancelled what might have been a romantic evening.

With the boy on the next farm, we arranged to take two interesting village girls to the Grange dance. He said he would drive. It was dusk and as the horse on the enclosed, doctor-type buggy was picking his way down the steep hill off the ridge, the foolish animal scared a skunk to the point of retaliation. The horse bolted, pulling the rig so fast that only a portion of the spray became attached to the horse, the rig and its occupants. But enough to create an emergency.

How to salvage an evening? Refusing to give up, the two drove into the village, at a fast trot, the few folks on the street running from the penetrating odor. We threw a young boy a quarter and told him to buy a bottle of cologne at the store. He obeyed, tossing a big bottle back to us and running off. We doused all of the contents over our hair, face and clothing—and smelled worse.

As we left the village for home, acknowledging defeat, we saw the girls. They laughed at us.

Our pal unhitched at his place and put the horse in a pasture field, running the buggy far from his house. Mother made us undress in the dark orchard behind the shed, scrub all over in tomatoes and their juice from her canned supply and then bury our clothes deep in the garden. Then, after a second tomato bath, she threw us a set of long johns and a night shirt and told us to sleep in the haymow. We do not recall how long it took us to once again become a member of the family.

One of the girls married our skunk-trip companion—long after he had been decorated.

PART III

Sixty Years a Newspaperman

Sixty Years a Newspaperman

MR. JENKS' ROME

We got along well, in our early days in the news gathering business, with our boss, Wooster Ohio Jenks, city editor of The Rome *Sentinel* for more than 50 years. Named for the city of his birth, he was a stern counselor, but usually kindly toward us. One of our personal responsibilities was securing for him a quart of "gin" weekly, in days of Prohibition. The supply could be short at times, but we always fulfilled that mission.

After a day's work—it began at 7:30 a.m. and ended at 4:30 p.m., then the time of publication, Mr. Jenks (he was never called anything else) liked to talk with young reporters. Going to school, we called it.

He wore a straw hat, in all seasons, at his rolltop desk, always taking it off when a female visitor came by. If it was someone who did not know Mr. Jenks' mannerisms, he often startled the caller with a loud and gruff, "and what do you want?"

When off-duty talk began, Mr. Jenks would deposit the straw hat on the flat desk behind him, relax and swing around in his chair. That hat was like a signal flag—on, it was all business—off, let's chat. He was a giant of a man, made all the more imposing by his larger than normal bald head, and his stern bearing, created by a stiff spine, caused by a bicycle accident. Those who knew him well enough twitted him about having fallen off his bike when he tried to peddle and watch a pretty woman at the same time. He

95

growled when he heard that.

We recall, among many other things, his descriptions of old-time Rome. Like in the 1870s when being at the corner of George and Linden was almost in the country, the "business zone" radiating about four blocks from the corner of James and Dominick.

Gravel sidewalks had been replaced with "tar walks," probably forerunners of bithulitic pavement. Some streets were flanked by flagstone walks and cobblestone gutters. Some inner district streets were paved with cobbles.

Nearly all the residences on the outskirts were surrounded by wooden fences; cattle and sheep were driven on the streets to slaughter houses. Homes were heated by wood or coal; water came from individual wells; the municipality maintained several public pumps.

Mr. Jenks said people in his childhood days had breakfast between 6 and 6:30 a.m., many businesses opening at 7 a.m. Some families kept sides of beef and pork hanging in ice houses in the back yard.

Flour came in barrels, as did crackers, and butter in tubs. The winter's supply of potatoes and other vegetables were kept in cellars, just as on any farm of those days. The wash tub used for the Monday laundry had been the family bath tub Saturday night.

According to Mr. Jenks, harmless green snakes were plentiful within the city, especially the cemetery, then at the site of present Fort Stanwix Park. Policemen walked their beats at night and the town bell called out volunteer firemen.

Men wore beards and barbers did their best business on Sunday afternoons. They called at homes to trim children's hair and that of old-timers unable to get to their shops.

Women braided their hair or wore it with a knot on top, in those days of bustles and of skirts that trailed in the dust. Only Indians painted their faces, Mr. Jenks said.

Carpenters and other skilled craftsmen earned a dollar, some a dollar and a quarter, a day. Poor people of the town called at kitchen doors of the rich for handouts.

The Black River Canal was the favorite swimming hole, particularly at the lock behind what is now Franklyn's Field. The livery stables were public forums and much of the entertainment was provided by traveling troupes that played the two local theaters.

Mr. Jenks could go on for hours about old-time Rome. These are but a few of our recollections of listening to this grand old man, to whom we owe so much for whatever success we have had in journalism. Little did we know then that we would be at The *Sentinel* longer than he and that, like him, we would be writing a local column for 18 years.

It is written in Durant's *History of Oneida County* that the first court held in Oneida County (formed in 1798) was called to order in a church in the township of New Hartford, Judge Henry Staring presiding.

He is described as a plain, honest Dutch farmer, a resident of German Flatts (Herkimer) and of limited education, but with a large stock of common sense.

The day was cold and the church had no heat. In the absence of warmth some of the lawyers induced the sheriff, an Irish veteran of Fort Stanwix named Colbraith, then residing between the Great Carry and what is now the hamlet of Stanwix, to produce a jug of spirits. This was quietly circulated and the court was persuaded to ignore the cold and to continue to dispense warm justice.

DRUMS ALONG THE MOHAWK

At dinner with Walter Edmunds at the Griffiss AFB Officers' Club, we asked if he liked the movie version of his great historical novel, *Drums Along the Mohawk*.

He was not enthused with what, 30 years after our conversation, has become one of the grand old-timers on late night television. Too many errors, he said, too much liberty taken with the truth.

The movie does not follow history. It does not abide with the story told in Edmunds' famous book. For instance . . .

Fort Dayton was located at present Herkimer, across the Mohawk River from and west of Fort Herkimer. The locale of Henry

Fonda's cabin in the movie was Deerfield.

In the picture, Fonda runs from Fort Herkimer to Fort Dayton to get help for settlers besieged south of the Mohawk. Closely pursued by Indians, it is one of the most exciting parts of the film. This chase undoubtedly was suggested to the script writers by the famous 30-mile run of John Adam Helmer, a famous hero of the Valley. He warned the settlers of the approach of Joseph Brant and his braves, a warning which allowed the pioneers time to congregate at Fort Herkimer before the war party arrived.

Helmer and two other white scouts encountered the Indians near Edmeston, about 15 miles south of Bridgewater. Helmer's companions were killed but he raced up the Unadilla Valley, outdistancing the Indians. After the war Helmer moved to Cayuga County and is buried near Weedsport.

Fort Herkimer, named for Jost Herkimer, father of General Nicholas Herkimer, was built in 1756 around Jost Herkimer's stone trading post. Herkimer Church is nearby, a short distance from Route 5-S, a few miles east of the Village of Mohawk. It is the oldest religious edifice in the Mohawk Valley.

In the movie, General Herkimer, mortally wounded at Oriskany, is brought to Fort Herkimer to die. This takes liberty with the truth, not unusual in so-called historical movies.

The general died at his homestead, still standing three miles southeast of Little Falls, about midway between that city and Indian Castle Church, on the Mohawk's south bank. The house was built in 1764 and is now the center of a state park. The bed of the old Erie Canal passes its yard facing the river.

Herkimer died 10 days after Oriskany, following the clumsy amputation of a leg.

Sure bets, if you need money: Wager that geese can't fly in the rain, that ducks can't walk without bobbing their heads, donkeys can't bray without raising their tails, and that most people can't sneeze without closing their eyes.

FIRST STARS AND STRIPES

Mention of new information concerning the early days of the Stars and Stripes vibrates quick nerves around Rome. So when we found a piece in a prestigious magazine (*Scientific American*, April 1988) about an archaeological find in New Jersey relating to the flag we thought: "Here we go again!"

But there was nothing there to challenge Rome's claim to be the place where the flag was first flown in the face of an enemy, a belief which grips serious historians of this region.

Titled "The Oldest Glory," the article relates the finding, during excavation of a Revolutionary War site at Pluckemin, New Jersey, of two metal plates (perhaps belt buckles) bearing what the magazine calls "the earliest known depiction of the American flag." That we challenge.

The archaeological project is on land where General Henry Knox quartered more than 1,000 troops between December 7, 1778 and early June of 1779. The Fort Stanwix flag flew in August of 1777.

One of the plates was on the surface, the other just under the ground. At first, it was thought these may have been "planted" there, but chemical analysis showed them to be of the same content as pieces of brass excavated elsewhere on the site, this seen as proof of their being contemporary with the Revolutionary War encampment.

The plates have an engraved image of a cannon (which, to us, seems more modern than those of the Revolution) and a flag, both of which have 13 stars while one flag has 14 stripes, the other 12.

Where we quarrel with the article is in its statement that these metal plates are the first to bear an image of the Stars and Stripes. The magazine declares that the earliest previous depiction of the flag dates from July of 1779, according to the Journal of Maj. John Ross, and that the earliest flag flown during battle was at Guilford Court House, in North Carolina, in 1781.

Local tradition is that the first Stars and Stripes was flown in the face of an enemy August 3, 1777, during the siege of Fort Stanwix, on the site of present Rome, New York.

To challenge the statement as to "the earliest depiction," being sometime between December of 1778 and June of 1779, there is the powder horn of Lt. Chris Hutton, adjutant of the Third New York Continentals, part of the garrison of Fort Stanwix when the flag was raised on the fort's southwest bastion that morning of August 3, 1777.

His powder horn, marked "Fort Schuyler" and with the date 1777, shows a "depiction" of a flag with stripes and a canton with stars—the first Stars and Stripes in action! (It is now in the collection of the Montgomery County Historical Society.)

In 1975, when the question of the first flag flown in the face of an enemy arose, Jerry D. Wagers, then North Atlantic regional director of the National Park Service (Boston), told us, in writing:

"We have no intention of challenging the Fort Stanwix flag tradition for it is every bit a part of the history of Rome as the Fort itself."

(Those desiring more information on this subject are referred to Edward C. Ball's "First Stars and Stripe to Defy Foe Flown at Fort Stanwix.")

This did not happen in a Rome court:

A defense lawyer asked a witness whose objectivity he was trying to challenge: "Is it not true that you are not an unbiased, objective witness because you, too, were shot in the fracas?"

"No, sir," declared the witness. "I was shot midway between the fracas and the belly button."

WHO WON AT ORISKANY?

The British invaders won the Battle of Oriskany, August 6, 1777?

That's heresy around the region of Fort Stanwix. It is holy writ that the successful defense of the fort and the American victory at Oriskany made possible the defeat of the British at Saratoga, the turning point of the American Revolution.

That's not the view of British and Canadian historians who insist the British Loyalists and their Indian allies won at Oriskany. (No British regulars or Hessian troops fought there.)

At the risk of being burned at the stake, we can see some merit in their claim. But read us out.

The Loyalists and Indians prevented the Mohawk Valley militia from raising the siege of Fort Stanwix. After the bloodiest battle of the Revolution, for numbers engaged, the Patriot militia was badly injured and forced to withdraw down the Valley, its usefulness shattered for the 1777 campaign.

These citizen soldiers were not driven from Oriskany. The Loyalists, those Americans of the Mohawk Valley who remained faithful to their King, and their Indian auxiliaries drew back from the fight after six hours of fierce, often hand-to-hand, neighbor vs. neighbor combat, leaving the field to the Patriots.

The British claims of victory rest on the undisputed fact that General Herkimer's men and boys were blocked, too shattered to continue on to the fort, only five miles away.

There were no American boasts of victory immediately after the battle. Gloom was thick in the Mohawk Valley. Scarcely a Patriot home had not lost family members at Oriskany. Fears of invasion were intensified. So concerned became higher headquarters at Albany that a stronger column of veteran troops was started up the Valley to the relief of the Fort Stanwix garrison and to prevent further penetration by the invaders. That relief force found no great numbers of the militia willing to return to the strife.

American claims to victory came after Saratoga and deserved attention. They were based mainly on three points—that the militia held possession of the field at Oriskany, that the Loyalists and their Indians had suffered morale-shattering losses, and that the battle had made possible a sortie from the fort that captured an Indian camp at the Lower Landing Place—this and the heavy casualties discouraging St. Leger's Indians to the point of desertion, causing the British to retreat.

If Oriskany was a tactical victory for the British, it resulted in a strategic victory for the Americans.

No one questions the courage of most of the men who fought there, on both sides. Not all of Herkimer's 800 gathered around their wounded commander on the plateau west of the ravine after the ambush. Many of the 200 in the rearguard of the militia column panicked at first fire, to be tracked down and killed in flight. Skeletons were found months later as far as two miles from the field.

But of the 600 men and boys, civilians, not soldiers, who fought for their homes in the woods of Oriskany, less than 400 were on their feet when the enemy withdrew.

Let historians on both sides add up the evidence and proclaim their views. The men who fought there—on both sides—left a mark on history that cannot be erased.

We once knew a man, a learned one, who was willing to speak out on many subjects, including how to operate voting machines. You pull the levers down and then you put them back up, he would insist. As far as we know, no one even convinced him otherwise. He said he always voted a straight ticket.

GEORGE WASHINGTON AT ROME

George Washington once had in mind that he would like to own land around Fort Stanwix, which he described as "much celebrated for the fertility of its soil and the beauty of its situation." If he had made the purchase, the City of Rome could look back to the commander-in-chief of American revolutionary forces as its first landlord.

Washington was with his Continental Army in Newburgh in 1783, waiting for the signing of the Treaty of Paris to end the Revolution. On July 18 of that year, no pressing military matters at hand and the general, apparently bored with inactivity, began a 750-mile, 19-day trip, mostly by horseback, which took him to Albany, Lakes George and Champlain, Bemis Heights, Ticonderoga, the Saratoga mineral springs, Schenectady and up the Mohawk Valley to the battlefield of Oriskany and on to Fort Stanwix (Rome).

From the fort he went to Wood Creek to examine the ruins of Fort Bull (on the site of Erie Canal Village), then by an old Indian trail from Oneida Castle to present Waterville and on to Otsego Lake where he turned north to Canajoharie, from there back to his headquarters in Newburgh.

While on this journey, Washington joined with his companion, Governor George Clinton of New York, in exploring the idea of buying the "mineral springs at Saratoga" and part of the Oriskany Tract on which Fort Schuyler (Stanwix) stood.

This plan did not materialize but the two partners did buy "6,000 acres" adjoining the Fort Bull-Fort Stanwix Tract from Marinus Willett and his wife "amazing cheap." (Willett had been second-in-command at Fort Stanwix during the 1777 siege.)

The land acquired was a long, narrow section running diagonally from a short distance west of Fort Bull to the southern area of Oneida County.

Before beginning his upstate trip, Washington wrote to Congress, July 16, 1783: "Finding myself in most disagreeable circumstances here (Newburgh), I am resolved to wear away a little time in performing a tour to the northward, as far as Ticonderoga and Crown Point and perhaps as far up the Mohawk River as Fort Schuyler (Stanwix)."

Light on what may have been the real purpose of the tour comes in a letter written by Washington, from Mount Vernon, November 23, 1784, to Governor Clinton:

"I am sorry we have been disappointed in our expectation of buying the mineral spring at Saratoga and the purchase of that part of the Oeriskeney [sic] tract on which Fort Schuyler (Stanwix) stands but I am glad you have succeeded upon such advantageous terms in the purchase of 6,000 acres adjoining, for you have certainly obtained it amazing cheap."

General Washington had faith in the future of his country buying tracts of land in New York, Virginia, Kentucky, Maryland, Pennsylvania and Ohio. It required 50 years to carry out the provisions made in his will concerning the disposition of those vast properties.

★   ★   ★

STEUBEN'S MAPLE SYRUP

In 1791, when Thomas Jefferson travelled to Vermont, he became interested in maple trees and their sweet products, to the extent that he ordered 60 young trees sent to his Monticello estate in Virginia. They did not grow, Jefferson not knowing that hard maples do best on high ground that is studded with granite rocks. This is news to us, but that is what is said.

History has another account involving maples, Oneida County maples. When Baron von Steuben, Washington's drillmaster, was selecting his bonus land after the American Revolution, he was advised to take acreage on the hills in what became the township of Steuben. He was told that there grew huge maple trees from which the Indians had been gathering sap for many years, producing sweet liquid and sugar. The available land being high on a hill, Steuben was informed it would be easy to pipe the flowing sap from the hillsides down to a central processing center in the valley.

What he was not told is that the maple sap season is only a few weeks.

Brick Hasfield says nostalgia is a longing for the place you would not move back to.

THE CANAL OVER "THE CARRY"

Wood Creek, now an insignificant stream flowing west from Rome, left its imprint on the military records of this country. It was the supply line to the British frontier at Oswego and Niagara. British troop columns used the Wood Creek route to capture Frontenac (Kingston) and subdue the St. Lawrence Valley. In the American Revolution, the British under St. Leger, sought to come into the Mohawk Valley by the Wood Creek route, to be turned back at Fort Stanwix.

Many soldiers died of disease and hard labor along Wood Creek, some 500 after Bradstreet's raid on Frontenac in 1758, while Fort

Stanwix was being built. Their bones, never recovered, lend mystery to the decayed waterway.

Wood Creek had a succeeding momentous role (1783-1817) as the vital transportation link by water across the Appalachian Divide, after the Revolution. Only at the Carrying Place (Rome) was this possible, Wood Creek taking people and goods westward from this historic portage, on the only low level water passageway to the west, between the St. Lawrence and north Georgia.

George Washington came to the Carry in 1783, as the Revolution was winding down, and suggested there must be a better way of moving goods over the Carry than unloading boats and hauling cargoes overland to the waterway (Wood Creek) to the west. Governor George Clinton (his nephew, Governor DeWitt Clinton, would become the "father" of the Erie Canal) revived Washington's idea in 1791 and, the following year, led in the formation of the Western Inland Lock Navigation Company to build a canal across the Carry, from the Mohawk River to Wood Creek, through what is now the City of Rome.

Political and commercial pressures resulted in the formation of two canal companies, the Northern Inland Lock Navigation Company to connect the Hudson River with Lake Champlain and the Western Inland Lock Navigation Company to join the waters of the Hudson with Lake Ontario and to improve the crude route along the Mohawk and Wood Creek.

Surveys indicated that a waterway some 5,352 feet long would be required at the Oneida Carry (Rome), to cost an estimated 3,000 British pounds. Clearing Wood Creek from Fort Newport, where present West Dominick Street crosses the creek, to Oneida Lake would need another 1,000 pounds.

Work was started in 1793 on a canal around the barrier, at present Little Falls, alongside a rift at German Flatts (Herkimer), and over the Oneida Carry. This work halted in 1794 for lack of funds.

Additional money was raised by stock subscription and the first boats passed around the rocky obstructions at Little Falls, November 17, 1795. In the first two days, 8 large and 200 small craft navigated this canal, paying a total of 80 pounds, 2 shillings in tolls. Cargo capacity there was up to 32 tons per boat.

The Western Inland Canal began at the River about a mile east of Fort Stanwix, near the Lower Landing Place, a short distance southeast of the present Amtrak station in Rome, and followed generally the route of what was to be in later years the Erie Canal, to a point near Rome's George Street. There it ran parallel with, but closer to present Dominick Street than the later Erie route, between George and Madison Streets along the southern boundary of the future Rome Sentinel Company property. It connected with Wood Creek near what was to be the U.S. Arsenal, built in 1815.

The Mohawk was a few feet higher than the creek and locks were necessary at each end of the canal to prevent river water from rushing into Wood Creek and to maintain a constant canal level. This ditch was 32 feet wide, maximum, at the top and from 2½ to 3 feet deep. Locks were 73 feet long and 12 feet wide with a 10-foot lift at the Mohawk and an 8-foot lift at Wood Creek. Bricks from these locks today are in the walls of the Arthur law building at George and Court Streets.

It was Rome's first canal, not to be confused with the Erie, which was begun here in 1817 and completed across the state in 1825.

The Western Inland Canal eliminated the use of cumbersome wagons and sleds on the rough portage. In 1812, alone, more than 300 boats, some carrying 1,500 pounds, passed through this short waterway. Thousands, traveling to settle the West, used this passage from one watershed to another.

Once the waterway across the Carry opened, work shifted to Wood Creek itself, many of the loops in the twisting stream being straightened and other obstacles removed.

The Mohawk boats carried a square sail and were steered by a swing oar, making up to six miles per hour in good wind. In Wood Creek they were pushed by men using long poles or were drawn by horses or oxen walking in the stream.

In dry seasons, water was impounded in what later became Thron's Pond, being released to "flush" boats down Wood Creek in the water-parched part of the stream.

All this seems impossible to an observer of what is almost a dry creek bed these days. There was much more water in Wood Creek. It began as a brook in the Lorena area and alongside present

Route 26 (Turin Road), two miles north of the city limits, merging with Mud Creek, originating near Greenway, before reaching Fort Bull at the western end of the Carry. Mud Creek was cut off from the Wood Creek system by the building of the Barge Canal around 1912.

The Inland Canal-Wood Creek waterway was abandoned when the Erie Canal became operative in 1825. Wood Creek, so influential in military history and in the settlement of Ohio and Michigan, a small but most important stream providing a linking of eastern and western water systems, went from glamor to disrepute as civilization (?) settled on these parts.

In 1897, this historic creek became Rome's sewer, the city's waste being diverted into Wood Creek, which became a sluggish, open cesspool, the sewage often equaling the amount of water in the creek. This stinking mess resulted in annual payments by the city to land owners along its banks until, under pressure from the state, this condition was eliminated in 1931 by construction of a sewage plant east of the city, alongside the Barge Canal.

Today, as one goes to Erie Canal Village, they will find what is left of Wood Creek, now only a swampy place in thick underbursh. Those so inclined can close their eyes and go back for centuries, seeing scores of boats in Wood Creek, loaded with troops or with adventuresome pioneers on their way to a new life in the West. It was once a mighty stream.

Brick Hasfield says it can cost more to go to the hospital than it once did to go to medical school.

THE FIRST TOWN BOARD

It may be of some interest to report the first town meeting of what is now Rome—at the home of Ebenezer Clafin, on the first Tuesday in April of 1796.

It was voted . . .

That Daniel Haws build a good and sufficient pound for the

Town of Rome, near the dwelling of Benjamin Gilbert. That Matthew Brown build a good and sufficient pound for the Town of Rome, near his dwelling.

That hogs be a free commoner, if they have good and sufficient yokes on (that meant they might roam at will). That every man take care of his own rams.

At an extra town meeting, held November 30, 1801, it was voted . . .

That 10 dollars be allowed and be paid to any person or persons who shall kill any panther, wolf or wildcat within the Town of Rome, in case the person is not entitled to a bounty from a neighboring town, as well as for any of those noxouious [sic] animals which may be discovered and pursued into a neighboring town and there killed; which circumstances of the killing shall be proven to the satisfaction of one or more justice of the peace of Rome.

That a bounty of one cent be allowed and paid for each red squirrel and two cents for each gray and black squirrel, killed within the Town of Rome between November 30, 1801 and the following April 1, to be proven before any justice of the peace.

And that 50 dollars be raised in the Town of Rome for the encouragement of the destruction of wolves, panthers, crows, jays and blackbirds.

★　　★　　★

Rome's first municipal water system was a hand-dug well, equipped with a "town pump," at the intersection of James and Dominick Streets, later the Busy Corner, more popularly called the American Corner, after the American Block.

This well was in operation prior to 1800 and was equipped with a trough, where cattle and horses were watered. It was surrounded by a curb to protect the pump from being damaged by horse and ox-drawn wagons. Later, village wells were in operation at Washington and Dominick and James and Embargo Streets.

★　　★　　★

ROME BEAUTY APPLES

The Rome Beauty apple, some say, has been reduced from a specialty ranking to standard, all-purpose listing. It no longer is a mystery as to name.

In 1813, Mr. and Mrs. Joel Gillette and their children, Alanson and Chloe, left Rome, New York, for the west, stopping at Marietta, Ohio, before journeying down the Ohio River to the wide bottom lands of Lawrence County, Ohio. Here they joined fellow Quakers in forming the township of Rome, Ohio, in an area formally called Quakers' Bottom.

Come 1817, the Gillettes ordered several fruit trees from upriver Marietta friends. Among them was a runt apple tree which Joel gave to his little son. Alanson set it out in the lush loam on the bank of the Ohio where it grew to produce the finest flavored apples known in the valley. People came from afar for graftings from the now famous tree.

In 1830, fruit growers believed "the Gillette apple" should have a national name. George Waldron, a neighbor, suggested "Rome Beauty" and the name was formally recorded on the records of the Ohio Convention of Fruit Growers.

It now ranks among the top in national productivity. The original tree was 40 years old in 1857 when it toppled from the eroding bank into the Ohio River.

Brick Hasfield says never plant a bigger garden than your wife can hoe.

THE GRAND OLD ERIE

Nearly 90 per cent of the necessary land for the Erie Canal was donated by far-sighted interests anxious to open up their holdings along its route. The net cost of construction was $7,143,789 and for the Champlain division $875,000. All of this was met by tolls and canal bond taxes within eight years.

In its first full year of operation, from Lake Erie to the Hudson River in 1825-26, more than 19,000 boats and rafts took passage. Land values along the canal rose $100,000,000 within five years, the population soared and the West (that land beyond Buffalo) became a viable part of the nation.

It cost $100 and took 20 days to move a ton of grain from Buffalo to New York City prior to the canal, over a poor road system. That dropped to $7 and $8 a ton and required only eight days, on the Grand Erie Canal.

It was dug and operated by the State of New York, without federal assistance, and without licensed engineers and power tools. It was the construction masterpiece of the 19th Century.

When you think of it, the American Indians did get a lousy deal. They are the only people conquered by the United States who didn't improve themselves at the expense of the victor.

FIRST TRAIN IN ROME

The first railroad train in Rome arrived, from Utica, Thursday, June 27, 1839, to be greeted by a large crowd whose enthusiasm was enlarged by the booming of a cannon. It continued on to Syracuse, returning to Utica, with a stop in Rome, in the early evening.

The Rome station of the Utica & Syracuse Railroad, a frame building painted yellow, stood on the later site of the old New York Central depot off South James Street, now occupied by the American Hardwall Supply Co. In time there were three depots there, the first wooden structure being replaced by a stone building which, in turn, gave way to the present one.

The single track line ran through the Great Rome Swamp (now the mucklands) on rails resting on a bridge-like structure which was supported by long piles driven into the wet, swampy ground. It was like an elevated railway in that section.

The Utica & Syracuse was Rome's first, but not the first upstate.

The Auburn & Syracuse had been operating for two years and the Utica & Schenectady for three prior to 1839. Eventually these were united to become the New York Central which, in 1914, moved its main line out of and to the south of the central district of Rome.

Brick Hasfield says a buffet supper is one where the guests outnumber the chairs.

THE LAMPLIGHTER

In the mid-1800's the gas lamps on Rome streets were not lit on those nights when the moon was full. That we read in old files of *The Rome Sentinel*.

We have only a hazy recollection of the old man who went about the village, down from Potato Hill, lighting the wicks of four big post-mounted oil lamps in the center of that community. Their total illumination would not equal that of one modern street light.

The village folks were proud of those lamps, the gift of a leading citizen. Probably other villages lit up like the town we knew in growing-up days. We are not talking, with tongue in cheek, about a communal beer blast. There wasn't any of that.

The lamplighter was a harmless village character, always boasting about how many rebels he had captured in the Civil War. Grandpa said the closest he got to that war was as a guard in the infamous Elmira prison camp.

But he knew his lamps. He'd push his wheelbarrow, loaded with a short ladder, a can of coal oil and some grimy rags, to the center of the village and he'd keep his chimneys as bright as those of any local housewife. As he cleaned his lamps, he told great tales for wide-eyed lads who followed him about, of voyages to far-off places, of combat in the war, of wicked big cities. We never could believe he was untruthful.

HISTORIC STANWIX HALL

There are citizens in this area with no remembrance of Stanwix Hall. It disappeared in the "Great Come Down" of Urban Renewal more than a decade ago.

The early structures on the site of Stanwix Hall (South James and Whitesboro) dated to around the 1840's. The area to be occupied by Stanwix Hall, a hotel, was used for a stove store at the corner and a small hotel next door on Whitesboro Street. It was a prime location, adjacent to the Rome harbor on the relocated Erie Canal.

Stanwix Hall went back to 1845 when the first hotel was demolished and a brick structure with ornate roofline was erected. This was modified, remodeled, renovated and enlarged several times, once being connected by an elevated passageway to Sink's Opera House on East Dominick Street.

Famous men knew Stanwix Hall. It was one of the finest stops in upstate New York along the Erie Canal. Politicians gathered there even before the Civil War. Teddy Roosevelt, running for president, rebuked young hecklers when he spoke from an iron balcony off the second floor, facing South James. "Go home, you rascals, where you belong," he shouted at them. News reports of the day gave no indication of their obedience.

Over the years, political groups of various varieties met there. In the 1920-30's, Stanwix Hall was a center of the community.

One of the last bigtime political figures to use Stanwix Hall was Robert F. Kennedy, when he was campaigning for the Democratic nomination of his brother, John, for the presidency. We remember it well. Bob Kennedy telephoned the editor of The *Sentinel*, in the early morning of September 19, 1960, to say he was coming up to see us. Realizing that the appearance of a Kennedy would interrupt newspaper production—all politicians liked to tour plants shaking hands—we said we'd come down to Stanwix Hall.

Told at the desk that Bob Kennedy and an aide were in a second floor room, we went up in the old elevator and knocked on the door. A voice said; "Come in."

Our introduction to a famous political personage was unique. The bathroom door was open, the place visible from the entrance.

The man we saw sitting on the toilet looked up and said he would be out in a moment. It was Robert Kennedy.

We had a short conversation, Kennedy asking if his brother Jack would carry Rome. We said he would—one time when a personal political prediction came true.

Later, when we accompanied Bob Kennedy down to the lobby where he spoke to a crowd of local Democratic faithful, he told of our visit, and lauded The *Sentinel* as "a good newspaper, with a fine editor." Ironically, the local Democratic organization was not thinking kindly of the local newspaper at that time.

Several years after, when, with Our Lady, we were at the Hickory Hill home of Robert Kennedy, with other New York editors, he recalled, with a laugh, the manner in which he had welcomed us to his Stanwix Hall room. For us, he was the best Kennedy of the lot.

Later we mentioned Stanwix Hall to new neighbors and they asked, "Where's that?" Realizing that newcomers have no conception of the old downtown, we said, "About where the city Christmas tree is raised on Fort Stanwix grounds. A short block south from the American Corner."

"Where was the American Corner?" The geography lesson went on for quite a while.

Brick Hasfield says ignorance is when you don't know something and somebody finds it out.

RAILROAD IN THE GORGE

Thousands motor through the Rome-Boonville Gorge these days, admiring the scenery and noting the many locks of the old Black River Canal—never noticing the remaining traces of what was to have been the Ogdensburg, Clayton & Rome Railroad.

It is an interesting story, although not so for the taxpayers of the then township of Rome and others along the way.

In the year prior to 1853, there arose a need for transportation north from Rome, to provide more rapid movement than was then available on the Black River and the Black River Canal.

In that year, there was formed a company to build a railroad linking Rome with Boonville, Carthage, Philadelphia (N.Y.), and Clayton, connecting the Erie Canal with the St. Lawrence River. Henry A. Foster, lawyer and former U.S. senator, was president; H.J. Beach, secretary, and R.D. Doty treasurer, all of Rome. They persuaded financial support from the people and the townships along the way, more than a million dollars being pledged, a tremendous amount in those days. A tenth of this was in hand before construction started.

It was decided to grade the rail bed throughout its extent before laying track, a mistake that doomed the project.

The railroad ran into a national depression, the company received no income from any operating sections along the route. And, worst of all, a rival line, the Utica & Black River, was being constructed from Utica to Clayton along the route of the present Conrail line to Boonville. Before the Rome-Clayton company began laying rails, the Utica & Black River had a steaming locomotive in Boonville. The Rome project was abandoned, with heavy loss to stockholders, including $60,000 in bonds issued by the town of Rome, a debt that lingered for years.

Traces of the right-of-way in the Gorge may be seen winding along the side of the hill on the western side of the highway, north of North Western. The engineers used the conventional method of railroad construction along a hilly course—curve out a grade on the slope of the hill, push rocks and dirt to one side as fill.

There is a tunnel on the route, through the "elbow" of the hill just north of the curve at Pixley Falls. It is filled in at both ends, to block off the inquisitive. (As this is written there are plans for a modification of this curve.)

Old newspaper accounts report that is was years before the town of Rome and other municipalities along the route finished paying off bonds they had issued to assist the never-to-be railroad.

★   ★   ★

Brick Hasfield says tough times don't last, tough people do.

★   ★   ★

CHURCH SUPPERS

The high point in the "supper season" is the last few weeks before election. Previous to days of electronic communication, politicians attended as many suppers as they could, often three or more a night in order to greet and press the flesh of as many people as possible.

Church suppers—the all encompassing term for the delightful, home-cooked meals served by organizations seeking to raise money for worthy causes—have always been a bargain. Once you could eat your fill for $1; times change and so do prices. Now the suppers are $4.50 and $5, even more.

One of the delights of such meals comes after the main courses, when they clean the tables, leave the fork and ask what kind of pie you'd like. We once wrote that one of our legitimate aims in life was to eat at a two-fork church. The next time we appeared for the supper at the Westernville Methodist Church the ladies in waiting marched down to our seat with two forks!

We suspect that the high standards of home baked pies are violated now and then with the intrusion of the "boughten kind" but, again, we are not complaining. A pie is a pie is a pie when they are scarce at home—for illogical reasons having to do with "health."

But let it be known, if ever the good women who labor so hard to raise a bit of money through the expertise of their natural talents begin to substitute new-fangled commercial forms for their home-cooked turkey, chicken, hams and beef roasts, we will have lost faith in womankind. We refuse to retreat from the search of excellence in home cooking as we scan the ads in the paper for the "church suppers."

We've heard is said that the honeymoon is over when she starts wondering what happened to the man she married and he starts wondering what happened to the girl he didn't.

WHY ROME IS A CITY

The history of the maneuvering which led to the chartering of the Village of Rome as the City of Rome, February 23, 1870, is fascinating reading. Few of recent generations have appreciation of the intense rivalry of those days between the political forces of Rome and Utica.

The paramount motivation that sparked Rome's civic establishment and its political leaders to seek city status was to gain more equal representation with Utica in the Oneida County Board of Supervisors. The Township of Rome had one seat in the board. The City of Utica had seven.

As one Roman put it then, "The Town of Rome with its population of 12,000 (the census figure for 1870 says 11,000) has but one voice in the Board of Supervisors, while the City of Utica, with 23,000 population, has seven to speak for her and to look after her interests."

The political facets of those days were well recognized in both communities. Rome was a staunch Democratic place; it had twice voted against Abraham Lincoln for president. Utica, a city since 1832, was strongly Republican. Additional supervisors from Rome were certain to be Democrats. The Republicans, who had a narrow edge in county government, feared a possible Democratic takeover should Rome gain additional political clout.

Adding irritation to an already fiery situation was a dispute between Rome and Utica over the location of a new office for the county clerk, a decision to be made by the Board of Supervisors.

Rome Democrats began agitating for a city charter prior to 1868. Rome Republican leaders objected continuously, but, being in the minority, could only make their voices heard.

The Civil War ended in 1865 with local political nerves still raw. One local Democrat became so aroused during the charter controversy that he declared, in public print: "Rome was a village when Utica was only a swamp!"

The State Legislature was divided in 1868, Republicans controlling the Senate, Democrats the Assembly. In this situation, early Rome city charter bills died in Senate committee.

Then in 1868 the Democrats captured the Senate and controlled the Legislature. The Rome city charter bill passed quickly.

Rome incorporated the entire township as a city, to gain as many county seats as possible. The former village was divided into four districts with a fifth supervisor representing the balance of the township. The current inside-outside municipal system dates back to that time.

Unexpectedly, a serious dispute arose between the two Rome political areas, the outside district muttering about unfair taxation and lack of services. A compromise, details now lost in history, ended a threat of secession.

Even as Rome Democrats were proclaiming that no longer would Rome play second fiddle to Utica, the Republican bosses of the larger city increased its supervisory allocation from seven to nine, partly offsetting the Democratic strategy.

After a few years of political maneuvering, the problem lost some of its fire although both parties sought support from rural towns to gain county control. Some say the struggle still goes on.

Brick Hasfield says one of life's ironies is that by the time a man has money to burn the fire has gone out.

ROME IN THE CIVIL WAR

The coming of the American Civil War was not totally unexpected by the 6,246 residents of Rome, New York.

Tension had been growing long before the 18th of February, 1861, when the train taking Abraham Lincoln to Washington to become President passed through the village. The political contest leading to Lincoln's election over a divided Democratic party had turned Romans against Romans. Daniel E. Wager, eminent Rome historian-editor, wrote of the local political war of that time:

"In addition to the writing of the editors (of the Democratic *Weekly Sentinel* and the Republican *Roman Citizen*), the politicans on both sides turned the vials of their wrath, ridicule and sarcasm into the columns of the respective newspapers, and each was a seething, boiling cauldron. The Rome newspapers carried on bitter, unrelenting personal and political warfare. A grand jury did not meet in this country that it was not besieged to find a bill of indictment for libel by the friends of each paper against the other."

Yet, as the war clouds darkened, only a few abolitionists talked in Rome about freeing the slaves. That was not a basic issue in the early days of that war. When Susan B. Anthony (today there's an unused coin in her honor) and a group of abolitionists attempted to lecture in Rome against slavery in early 1861, they were shouted down by a mob and forced to leave town.

Lincoln did not speak in Rome; his train did not stop. There were Romans in the crowd in Utica—estimated by Republicans as "around 10,000"—when he made a short speech: "I appear before you to bid you farewell, to see you and to allow you to see me. At the same time I acknowledge, ladies, that I think I have the best bargain in sight. I only appear to greet you, and to say farewell." A reporter described him as "tall and gaunt."

When Confederate batteries opened fire on Fort Sumter in the Charleston, South Carolina harbor, April 12, 1861, Rome was a busy village, an agricultural center with a few basic industries. It was served by the busy Erie Canal and two railroads, the New York Central and the Rome, Watertown & Ogdensburg, the Central running 12 passenger trains daily and the RW&O four.

The village extended to Wright Street on the south, to Expense Street on the west, to Garden on the north and to what is now Third Street to the east. The present corner of Turin and George was on the outskirts.

There were no stores on Dominick Street west of Washington, except for a grocery at the corner of Madison. On the east side of North James Street, there were only two shops north of Willett, then called Stone Alley.

There were no flagstone sidewalks outside the business section; some of the walks in front of the stores were plank and some of the downstreets were paved with cobblestones. All else was hard-packed dirt, except in early spring when mud took over.

The Erie Canal had been in full operation since 1825, the New

York Central Railroad since 1839. It was only 32 years since the last trace of Fort Stanwix had been covered, 78 years after the end of the American Revolution. A few veterans of that war were alive.

Seven plank roads radiated into the countryside. Stages ran daily between Rome and Boonville, Lee Center, Hamilton and Turin.

The village had gas street lights, which were turned on only when the moon did not shine. There were five banks, about 600 dwellings and 60 shops. Within the village limits were two steam-powered planing mills, two furnaces, two breweries, a sawmill, two blind and door shops, three carriage factories, a candle and soap works and a grist mill, in addition to the artificial gas plant and factories producing shoes, farm machinery, household goods and railroad iron rails.

There were 12 churches, one Presbyterian, two Baptist, two Methodist, one Episcopal, two Roman Catholic, one Welsh Methodist, one Lutheran, one Universalist and one African Baptist. Eight hotels welcomed the traveling public, as did numerous saloons and boarding houses.

The village, incorporated in 1819, was nine years from becoming a city. Politically, the township of Rome was Democratic, turning its back on Abraham Lincoln, the Republican, both times he came up for election. He lost Rome 934 to 837 in 1860 and by 1,239 to 769 four years later.

Regardless of political feeling, Rome and its area supported the war effort as enthusiastically as any village in upstate New York, providing many of the men in the 14th and 26th Volunteer Infantry, called out early in the war, and in the 117th and 146th, raised in Rome and at the front in 1862. Numerous other organizations had Rome soldiers, including the 97th, organized in Boonville and at the front in March of 1862.

Many of the business places and homes in Rome, particularly near the New York Central tracks, which in those days ran through the village, were draped in mourning when Lincoln's funeral train passed through Wednesday, April 26, 1865—carrying the body of the man who had said in Utica, four years before: "I appear before you to bid you farewell."

★　★　★

JOKES AND JOKERS

This region has had its share of minor hoaxes—the pet woodchuck in Western that dug post holes on command, the old hunter in Old Forge who took deer alive with bullets soaked in nicotine, and, some say, our squirrel that forecasts winters by the way it carries its tail.

These are gentle folk tales compared with what some call the greatest hoax ever perpetrated on the gullible American people.

It was on October 16, 1869, that two laborers, digging a well for Stub Newell in Cardiff, south of Syracuse, uncovered the Cardiff Giant, an over-sized figure weighing 2,900 pounds and measuring 10 feet ½ inches in length. People came by buggy and on foot from miles around to see the Giant. As many as 3,000 viewed him in one day. Arguments flourished as to whether he was a prehistoric statue carved "to perpetrate the memory of a great mind and noble deeds" or whether it was a true-to-life fossil of a "big Injun."

It was a monstrous practical joke. George Hull, a relative of Newell, had the figure carved from Iowa gypsum and shipped in an iron-strapped box by train and wagon to central New York State. It was carted from the railroad depot to Cardiff and quietly buried one dark November night in 1868 behind Newell's barn. The site was seeded to clover and the figure was uncovered, by design, the following year.

The expert on humbug, P.T. Barnum, offered $69,000 (big money in 1869) for a three-month lease on the Giant, but was turned down. Not to be outdone, Barnum had a replica made which he advertised as "The Original of All Cardiff Giants."

The original changed owners many times during the next 50 years, making money for most of them.

Today the Cardiff Giant rests in peace at the Farmers' Museum in Cooperstown.

Hoax tales pop up year after year. Those of the body of the old lady in the casket strapped to the top of a car and the car is stolen; the man pulled over and off the roof when his wife drives out of the driveway in the car to which he has attached his safety rope; the cement driver who fills his wife's lover's convertible with fresh concrete; the lady who dried her poodle in the microwave oven; the substitute milkman who is punched by the jealous husband, and the naked husband sleeping in the trailer who rolls out when his wife slams on the brakes at a red light and then drives away leaving him in the street, with no identification.

Readers may seek to add the Empeyville Frog, whose croaks sound like dynamite explosions as far away as Rome and who empties many a pond by just leaping into it. But there are those who stoutly maintain that the Frog is not a hoax and are ready at any time to defend its existence. For us, the Frog is real. We've had too many totally trustful people tell us they have seen it.

And, of course, our weather-telling squirrel is on the up and up. It just happens that we are the only one who is acquainted with it.

Brick Hasfield says never hire an electrician with scorched eyebrows.

OUR SURE-TAILED SQUIRREL

Anyone involved with local column writing is besieged with good-intentioned advice as to the weather of the forthcoming winter. For that reason, we depend only upon the signal from our forecasting squirrel who indicates what each winter will bring by the manner in which he holds his tail in late fall.

We have never disputed other signs. Those who insist upon checking the thickness of a pet horse's hair, the depth of a corn husk, or the coat sported by a caterpillar should preserve their own faith.

For years we have been hearing that thick corn husks, long-haired horses and darkly uniformed worms are dependable for the purpose. We can only say that for over 18 years, our squirrel has been correct as to the state of winter 78 per cent of the time. That, we submit, is about on a par with experts equipped with all the latest electronic gadgets.

It is too much work searching for caterpillars, seeking to inspect a horse in this motor car age and invading corn fields. It is much easier to glance at one's talented squirrel and note how it is carrying its tail—straight up, a good winter; straight back, easy winter; tucked between the ears and pointing in the direction the squirrel is going—watch out!

Indian Joe, up St. Lawrence way, used other methods. If black squirrels were swimming the river in the fall, from Canada to the U.S., he'd say the rodents knew what was coming down from the north. He explained his best vision of what was ahead by saying he knew it would be a tough time when "white man put up big piles of wood."

The *Sentinel* once had a police reporter who declared that a woman reporting a burglary said she did not suspect anything was wrong when she discovered all the drawers in the bedroom were open and the contents scattered about. "I thought my husband had been looking for a clean shirt."

★   ★   ★

THE LADY IN PANTS

We have always been glad that Rome can boast that Dr. Mary Walker once practiced here, at 76 West Dominick Street, with her husband, Dr. Albert Miller. That is, until the partnership, professional and matrimonial, broke up when she questioned his fidelity, he admitting the offense and offering to grant her the same privilege.

And we were happy when the Army restored Dr. Mary Walker's Congressional Medal of Honor. It didn't do her much good, she having been dead since 1919 and actually never gave up the Medal—which she proudly wore after the Army wrongly scrubbed her from a list of heroes, along with 909 others.

She gained much notoriety because she insisted on wearing men's clothing even when she served in the Civil War as a contract surgeon, including four months as a prisoner of the Rebels.

Dr. Mary was much her own self in all things, insisting on wearing trousers at her wedding and deleting the promise "to honor and obey" from the ceremony. When she obtained her final divorce decree in 1869, she is reported to have said, in high glee: "Divorce and the last of the villian!"

Brick Hasfield says most men believe in heredity until their kids start acting goofy.

THE EMPIRE HOUSE

It was fascinating to read in the August 23, 1870 *Sentinel* that the "valuable house and lot" on East Dominick Street, "for the past six years occupied as a seminary (by Miss M. J. Whittemore) and formerly the residence of H. A. Foster" was up for sale at auction.

This was the famous Empire House, the oldest structure in Rome when it was demolished to make way for the Fort Stanwix National Monument. It stood from the very beginning of the 19th century at what in later days was designated as 111 East Dominick Street. Its unique history included use as a frontier tavern close by the ruins of Fort Stanwix, a law office, a school, a temporary church, a parsonage, a residence and a picturesque saloon, not necessarily in that order.

A portion of it, the eastern wing, was built over the filled-in ditch (dry moat) around the fort, according to accounts by Joshua Hathaway, who saw the fort before it was leveled prior to 1828.

After being used, before 1808, by Presbyterians for church services and later as a parsonage, it finally became the Empire House, in 1896. When it was Joe O'Brien's place (father and son), the predominate topics over a grand old bar—no women permitted, free lunch one of the best in town—were politics, baseball and horse racing. That continued into our time; we remember well the hearty beef dinners, with pie, 35 cents.

One of the best stories about the Empire House is provided by a report in the *Sentinel*. It concerns a Stanwix man who started out with horse and cutter in a blinding blizzard. Hours later the horse and cutter were noted in front of the Empire House, the man unconscious on the seat. The horse, well acquainted with his owner's activities, had taken him to his destination. The driver was quickly revived, probably with something to which he was accustomed.

A delightful entry concerning Fort Stanwix appears in the Gates Papers, in the New York Historical Society archives:
". . . has built a house by order of the general for one Stefanny who is married to a squaw 24 ft. long by 12 ft. wide."

A DIFFERENT DOLLAR THEN

The Federal income tax, originating in 1862, had a rate in 1867 of 5 percent of gross income, after $1,000 exemption. Alfred Ethridge, wholesale grocer, paid $10,036, the highest in Rome, all taxes being published in the local papers.

One of the most popular doctors showed a tax payment of $1,113. The two *Rome Sentinel* publishers, A.C. Kessinger and F.B. Beers, reported $1,403 and $1,434, respectively.

It was a different dollar in 1867. Eggs were a quarter a dozen, Maine potatoes 60 cents a bushel. A big glass of beer, with free lunch, was a nickel and room and board could be obtained for $2 a week. Standard wages for laborers was 60 to 80 cents a day.

Brick Hasfield says nothing disturbs domestic tranquility like having a wife say she can't remember whether she first saw that late TV movie with her husband or some other boy friend.

MORE BICYCLES THAN CARS

Rome was once a city of bicycles. In the 1920's and 30's, there were more bicycles on the streets than there were automobiles.

Roads and streets were often muddy, sidewalks were rough and bumpy. Bicycle clubs became popular, bringing political pressure upon the municipality to establish wider bicycle paths along prominent streets. Commissions were appointed to supervise the bike paths.

One of the most popular was alongside Floyd Avenue, then over a crossroad to Ridge Mills and down James Street, with a connection from Turin Street. This was known as "the big horn." Fees were charged, in the form of bicycle tags, for use of such facilities. All this was at the turn of the century, in 1899-1905.

Brick Hasfield says California is not a bad place if you overlook its faults.

THE OLD LIVERY STABLE

In the late 19th century and for a few decades later the inhabitants of a small city kept horses in barns on local alleys. That was in days of trolley cars and bicycle paths, when without these you walked or drove a horse from place to place.

We knew a little about livery stables from accompanying our grandfather to town where he had a choice between tying his horse to a hitching post alongside the street or stabling it for a few hours.

Horse lore in our days was learned in the farm stables, a smaller structure attached to the big barn and containing stalls for four horses, space for a shop, ample room for surreys, buggies and cutters and with a hay mow under the slanting roof.

We learned early that on cold mornings you did not insert the bit into a horse's mouth without warming it in your hands. And we knew that you spoke to a horse before entering its stall.

In communities such as Rome, a young boy could become

acquainted with fascinating, and much more costly, things in the carriage houses on the alleys where town horses were stabled. There were the bull's-eye lanterns, buffalo robes, silver-handled whips, strap sleighbells and soapstones, with shiny harness hanging in place along the inner walls. The soapstones were heated, when one was driving on a cold day, and wrapped in old carpet for placement under the buffalo robe. We had such things on the farm, but not from such expensive stock.

Young boys were more welcome in carriage houses then in the downtown livery stables. Those great educational centers of the horse age were not partial to kids hanging around, livery stables being combinations of hack stands, rent-a-horse agencies, parking for visiting horses, carriages, harness and horse sales centers, and a 24-hour-a-day men's club.

Many years before supermarkets kept open 24 hours, livery stables had their lights on all night, a "swipe" sleeping on an office cot ready to take in a late night arrival, to hitch up the doctor's mare, or put a team on a combination ambulance-hearse.

There were worn decks of playing cards, dominoes and pitching horseshoes around. And, in some of the more thoughtful livery stables, there might be a bottle of whiskey hidden in a feed bin for sudden emergencies. "Rye for rattlers, bourbon for boredom" was a saying handed down to folks with little knowledge of life around horses in older days.

Country preachers often damned the livery stable as one of the community hell holes, on a par with the pool hall. Thoughtful grandmothers warned small boys never to be seen in such places although, in our time, we headed for them at almost every opportunity, seldom to be admitted without an accompanying adult male. We remember the cuspidors, burlesque queen calendars and the often overheard, but not understood jokes carried from town to town by traveling salesmen.

And the smells—they still linger. In those days communities, big and small, had the aroma of farmyards, the odors of fresh manure blended with the scents of corn, straw, tanbark, clover, hay and sweat-stained horse blankets and harness leather. And the smells of horses, in stables, at hitching posts, on packed dirt roads, clip-clopping on brick-paved main streets.

Mixed with the smells of those days were the flies. When the Rome Chamber of Commerce was originated, around 1912, one of its first projects involved enlisting children in a campaign of swatting flies, for monetary awards. The street sweeper, with his barrel on wheels, his shovel and his broom, was a familiar sight and an attraction for the flies.

The prevailing odors of those times were accepted as one of the costs of community living. Around the turn of the century, most city males knew more about living with horses than many farmers do today, some of them never having owned one.

Young ladies loved horses but, we imagine, not to ride after reading in a newspaper or magazine that horseback riding produced, as one authority put it, "an unnatural consolidation of the bones of the lower body, insuring a frightful impediment to future functions which need not here be dwelt upon."

Brick Hasfield says some children should be reprimanded for imitating their parents.

THE ARLINGTON HOTEL

We have a special interest in the Arlington Block, one of the handsome structures of Rome before Urban Renewal. Our first daughter, Shirley, was born there when it housed the Rome Infirmary.

Erected in 1875 by Don Pedro McHarg, Sr., it was first known as the McHarg Block, becoming the Arlington later after a hotel by that name was established there.

When W. M. & C. W. Buell ran the Arlington Hotel, they advertised in the 1889 directory: "Connected with the new Washington Street Opera House, eligibly located in central portion of the city; new, large, modern and commodious. Has 100 rooms with hot and cold running water, baths and elevator. Parlors and sleeping rooms large and well ventilated. Patent fire escape in every room.

Street cars run past the door every few minutes." (That patent fire escape probably was a long rope coiled in a box beneath a window.)

Don Pedro McHarg, Sr. was described by the *Rome Sentinel*, when he died in 1905, as "the type of man who pushes ahead." He was one of the original 49ers who went to California as a boy of 17 in the Gold Rush. He returned to Rome with considerable wealth, part of which he invested in the building that stood for nearly 100 years at Rome's Dominick and Washington Streets.

Brick Hasfield says the difference between genius and stupidity is that genius has its limits.

When the federal income tax was enacted into law, October 3, 1913, a senator, speaking in opposition, declared: "If we allow this 1 per cent foot in the door, at some future date it may rise to five per cent!"

Which reminds us that when the Fort Stanwix recognition legislation was before the U.S. Senate, in 1935, a senator in opposition, arose and declared: "Mark my words, if this bill becomes law they will be back asking for $30,000!"

Fort Stanwix National Monument dates back to this authorization of the commemorating, in an unspecified manner, of the famous fort on the Oneida Carry (Rome), a project whose cost ultimately was in excess of $7 million!

BEFORE OUR TIME

Once upon a time, around these parts . . .

If you had a liquor problem, you could take the Gold Cure at a sanitarium in Clinton which, the advertisement said, had treated more than 500 patients in the past 16 years.

If you wanted to rent a horse, M. Thalman could help you at the

Rome Livery & Boarding Stable, at 126-128 North James Street, at the intersection with Stone Alley. (It was later the Star Theater and even more recently, The Big Apple, before being demolished in the Big Tear-Down of Urban Renewal.)

If you had an urge for fish, oysters, clams or lobsters, they were usually available at George W. Sturdevant's lunch room, corner of Washington and Dominick Streets. Or, like fare could be found at J.M. Sturdevant's California Restaurant at 126 North Washington Street.

And if you were going out to dinner, you could see some of your acquaintances at the Gansevoort, operated by Grossman and Wolff, at 204 South James Street.

Of course, you'd have to have been here in 1893!

Brick Hasfield says it's necessary to have a good memory to be a good liar.

THE ROME & OSCEOLA RAILROAD

The Rome & Osceola Railroad never collected a fare or hauled a pound of freight. The only thing it carried in its brief years of corporate existence was the hopes of farmers and lumbermen in its territory and the aspirations of enterprising businessmen.

It was the brainchild of two Utica brothers, John D. and Pierpont White, who conceived it as a means of hauling lumber from their more than 21,000 acres of timber in the Osceola area. With the financial assistance of a number of wealthy residents of Oneida County, including a few Romans, they engaged engineers, in 1908, to chart a route for a railroad from Rome to the timberlands on Tug Hill. It was to operate on double tracks from a terminal on South Charles Street in Rome to Osceola, via Lee, Annsville, and Glenmore.

Work on the 35-mile railroad began in 1909, some 35 workmen, intermittently over nearly five years, grading and cutting out a right-of-way. They worked 10 hours a day, six days a week, assisted by a steam shovel operated on temporary tracks.

The project ran out of money in 1914, being purchased by a Pennsylvanian who sold to the Gould paper interests of Lyons Falls. A truck road was built into the Osceola timber country from the north and the need for a log railroad from the south declined. The company filed for bankruptcy in the early 1920's.

Traces of the right-of-way may be noted in several places. Sections of the bed of the railroad "that never was" have been found useful by snowmobilers.

These must have been Good Old Days—if one was making at least $15 a week . . .

When the *Saturday Evening post* sold for 5 cents a copy . . . when the savings banks of Rome charged 5 per cent on real estate mortgages . . . when you could rent a five-room flat on West Park Street with "water and sewer" for $5 a month . . . when local houses were advertised for sale "from $800 up."

And when 2,500 employees of four Rome industries—Rome Brass & Copper Company, Rome Tube Company, Rome Manufacturing Company and Rome Metal Company—were guests, with their families, of their employers at a dance in the new mill of Rome Metal Company, "east of Rome, three miles from the American Corner." (The *Sentinel* reported it was an "intoxicating event, held in the bar room of the new metal mill.")

Only real old-timers will recall, but these items from an old *Sentinel* present a picture of life in Rome in 1903 . . .

R. L. Utley, 200 West Dominick Street, would deliver a gallon of "12-year-old Pepper Whisky anywhere in the city" for $3.20.

The Cyclers' Skating Rink, on North Madison Street, was operating every afternoon and evening, with Yordon's Full Band Saturday nights.

The Oneida County Savings Bank, in its new quarters at 178

West Dominick Street and the Rome Savings Bank, 105 South James Street, were paying 3½ per cent interest on deposits and taking mortgages on houses and lots at 5 per cent.

W.H. Maxham, 156 West Dominick Street, advertised boys' velvet slippers for 29 cents; men's leather slippers for 47 cents; ladies' fur-trimmed Juliettes, 79 cents. Our future father-in-law was giving away an oak rocker every Wednesday, coupons included with every sale above 50 cents.

Corned beef rump 8 cents a pound, salt pork 9 cents a pound and three bottles of maple syrup or catsup for a quarter at The New York Grocery, 284 West Dominick Street. Oysters, "fresh from Virginia," were $1 a gallon.

Police Chief Barry had detailed Officers Beckwith and Conley to enforce the ordinance requiring bells on sleighs or horses.

No one had any idea that 40 years later big airplanes would be flying over the city from a military base in Rome.

★ ★ ★

Brick Hasfield says money isn't everything but it sure keeps you in touch with your children in college.

★ ★ ★

Remember . . .

When you could buy an ice cream freezer for $1.26?

A snap-on handle and three sadirons for 75 cents; an enameled teapot for half a dollar; a coffee grinder for 40 cents?

A stereoscope and 500 slides for $2.98; a talking machine for $40; a rocking chair for $3; a wooden ice box for $8.93 and a Parlor Gem Organ for $37.35?

If you do, you are either long in the tooth or you have been looking at a 1910 mail order catalogue.

★ ★ ★

Brick Hasfield says nothing makes it harder to tell the truth than a black eye.

★ ★ ★

SNATCHING SUCKERS

A piece in a March, 1891, Rome *Sentinel* caught our eye, reporting that "with the advent of each recurring spring, the sucker fishermen are at hand at the Mohawk River . . . At this time of year (early spring) the flesh of the sucker is very sweet and toothsome."

Catching suckers was part of our growing up. We were warned they were good for eating only in the springtime, but we patrolled the banks of the brook in spring, summer and fall, watching for the big suckers motionless in the clear water.

We were not unconventional when we ignored baited hooks for wire snares. It was common practice and exciting working a thin wire loop, attached to a fish line, around the motionless sucker and yanking when the loop was positioned just behind the gills, the fish falling on the bank. Snatching, it was called.

No one ever told us, at the age of five or six, that we were breaking the law. Ignorance is no excuse but a two-pound old sucker is to be remembered. The statute of limitations has run out.

Brick Hasfield says profanity is a public proclamation of stupidity.

ROME'S STREET CARS

With James and Dominick (the American Corner) as the hub, the Rome street car system, at its peak in the 1920's, operated lines on Dominick Street, on James-Thomas-Floyd, on North James, on Dominick-Expense-Kent, on Dominick-Madison, to the New York Central depot and, at one time, on loop lines connecting Expense and Madison via Thomas and Madison and James over Linden. Cars were stored in a large barn on John Street, with access to and from the American Corner over John and South James.

The first street cars in Rome—horse-powered—were put into service in 1887, when bicycles were the high-wheeled type. Those who did not own horses, and numerous families did, walked when they traveled in the city, then only 18 years old.

The first horse-car route was on Dominick, followed by service on North James. Cars were of two sizes, long ones pulled by a team, short ones by a single horse.

The first franchise was awarded by the Common Council around 1885 to the Haines brothers of New York City. They proposed a belt line from the railroad station, then on South James Street, up James to Turin, over Turin to Elm, along Elm to Madison, down Madison to Dominick and over Dominick to the American Corner and the depot. There was to be another line on Dominick Street from the Locomotive Works in East Rome to a point west of the Wood Creek bridge. A third route was scheduled over North James and Stanwix Streets to Floyd Avenue and on to Riverside Park (the old County fairgrounds, now Wright Park Manor).

The Haines firm did nothing with the franchise, which in 1887 passed to R.F. Hill and C.W. Dayton, also of New York City. They contracted with W.J. Cramond for erection of a car barn and stable on John Street, Cramond sub-letting the work to Carey & Burney. At the same time, on April 23, 1887, H.H. Hawkins of Lee was given a contract to purchase 60 horses.

The John Street building was to include stables, blacksmith shop, car sheds and passenger depot. George Schillner of Rome was the architect. In May of the same year, the original depot of the Rome, Watertown & Ogdensburg Railroad, which stood near the New York Central station on South James Street, was moved to John Street to be the street car ticket office and waiting room.

The first rails were laid May 22, 1887, on West Dominick Street, at Madison, the crews working both directions from that point, the western end of the line being extended to Doxtater. The trial run was made June 28, 1887 over John Street to James, to the American Corner, west on Dominick to Madison and up North Madison to Park Street. That was the beginning of street car service in Rome.

Horse cars were operated until the fall of 1900 when Hardie air motor cars were put into use, the first running on the Floyd Avenue line September 22, 1900. These operated with compressed air and did fairly well until June 12, 1902, when they were forbidden to use the condemned South James Street bridge over the Erie Canal to get to the compressors at the car barn. For the balance of that summer, horse cars were back in use.

In May of 1908, the Rome City Street Railway Company was sold to the Utica & Mohawk Railroad Company, which set out to electrify the Rome system. Trolley cars, taking energy from an overhead cable, began operating later that year and continued until December of 1930 when the days of street cars came to an end in Rome, motor buses taking over.

Those who remember the electric trolleys know how the small cars pitched, up and down from one end to the other, how one had to guard against sliding down the side seats to the end of the car and back and how, in winter, it was the trolley car plow-sweeper that opened paths in otherwise unplowed streets.

There was another trolley system, the interurban line connecting Rome with Utica and Little Falls. It went out of business in the 1930's, its bridge over the Barge Canal on Mill Street being put up for auction. This is the city-owned eastern span, the one that remained in use both ways until the problem with the western state-owned bridge was solved.

There is a tale of the restrictions of government in connection with that old interurban bridge. Richard Wilson, then commissioner of public works, was authorized by the Rome Board of Estimate and Contract to bid up to a cap of a few thousand dollars. A Utica scrap dealer went a few more dollars and Wilson, under his orders, could not pay more. The city then gave the dealer a good profit to secure the needed bridge. That caused a sharp political rumble in Rome.

★   ★   ★

Sometimes it is wise to look back to see better ahead. Here's what some experts said in the past:

"With over 50 foreign cars already on sale here, the Japanese auto industry isn't likely to carve out a big slice of the U.S. market."—*Business Week*, in 1958.

MUSEUM OF MEMORIES

We are surrounded by fond memories in the Clarence Harden Barn at Erie Canal Village. Almost every type of road vehicle that took us from place to place, from home to school and back, is on view in the Harden collection.

There are the horse-drawn sleds of winter, the farm bobs, the two-seater sleighs and the cutters, plain and fancy, all reminiscent of our childhood. We rode many miles in them during winter months, wrapped in a bearskin robe, a warm soapstone by our feet, to the village with grandparents to shop, to the neighbors for "visits," once, as we well remember, to the doctor to have a big neck boil lanced, probably bawling, going and coming.

And when we were older, we drove the road horse to school from our Dad's farm and to and from the dances in the Grange Hall in town.

Not to be forgotten is the surrey, yes, with fringe on top, which, while seldom used, was handy if the entire family wanted to go to the county fair, to church, to Memorial Day exercises, or even to an auction which would provide fun for adults and children alike, excitement to interrupt the often drab life of an uphill farm.

More sage hindsight . . .

"Television won't be able to hold on to any market after the first six months."—The head of 20th Century-Fox in 1946.

"1930 will be a splendid employment year."—U.S. Department of Labor, in 1929.

COBBLESTONE STREETS

The Rome area's first hard surfaced roads and streets were of stone, brick or planks (the latter, wooden highways laid by chartered companies authorized to collect tolls). There is undated documentation that Washington Street, in Rome, was planked from Dominick Street northward, how far is not stated.

There was a time when farmers living outside of Rome were encouraged to haul in cobblestones in their wagons, a service to them in getting rid of the obstacles and to the village which used the stones to pave muddy streets and alleys. Willett Street was once known as Stone Alley.

Such pavements were extremely hard on horses, the stones bruising their tender frogs. The cobblestones also had a way of jolting wheeled vehicles and making steel-tired wheels ring loudly. But they were preferable to deep mud holes on heavily-traveled streets.

There came a day when the mayor, Dr. W.J.P. Kingsley, paid out of his pocket for the first piece of brick pavement in Rome, in September of 1895, on West Dominick Street in front of the Willett Block, which he owned. Soon several neighbors on the street followed his example until finally the city was encouraged to brick the entire street, the beginning of a program which led to other brick streets and then to the use of asphalt and finally to bitulithic paving.

Brick Hasfield says dieting is what helps a fellow gain weight more slowly.

ROME'S ELECTION HISTORY

For 70 years, from 1900 through 1969, Rome had a reputation of being first with election returns, the result of an elaborate coverage system by the Rome *Sentinel*. The newspaper took great pride in having the Rome returns first on the Associated Press wire across the nation.

It accomplished this with election checkers and runners in all of the city's local districts. It was a long and great tradition.

Like the year the *Sentinel* announced six minutes after the polls closed that General Eisenhower, GOP candidate for president, had carried Rome. *New York Times* political reporters, in those early days, always stopped by Rome to see how the winds were blowing. Ex-Romans listening to election returns outside a newspaper office on the West Coast could safely wager that their home town would be the first to report from New York State.

Cub reporters were indoctrinated that no matter what else they were to be at their assigned voting place 10 minutes before the polls closed, pencil in hand to fill out the blank with which their "runner" would dash for the *Sentinel* office.

The first year we worked in this system, in 1927, we were driving to our assigned station with the Lady of Our House. Two blocks away the car stalled and began to smoke. What did we do? Call for help? Search for possible fire?

We ran to collect the returns, leaving our wife to seek whatever assistance she might find.

Brick Hasfield says this is a land of opportunity where anyone can grow up, get a job and go on unemployment insurance.

1903 RULES FOR TEACHERS

We came across these regulations laid on the 1903 school teachers in Birmingham, Michigan.

They were not to get married, not to keep company with men, to be in bed between the hours of 8 p.m. and 6 a.m. unless in attendance at a school function, not to linger in ice cream stores, not to leave town without permission of the chairman of the school board, not to smoke, not to drink beer, wine or whiskey, not to get into a carriage or automobile with any man except a brother or a father, not to dress in bright colors, not to dye their hair, not to wear less than two petticoats and not to wear skirts or dresses more than two inches above the ankle.

The teachers of that place and that day were sternly instructed to keep the classroom neat and clean, to sweep the floor at least once a day, to scrub the floor once a week with hot water and soap, to clean all blackboards daily and to have the stove in the room fired by 7 a.m. so that it would be warm for the children when they arrived at 8.

That profession had come a long way!

SURE CURE FOR SORE THROATS

Dr. Don Amidon, once our health consultant, sends along, without comment, an old paper placemat which calls attention to medical advice of Grandma's time. It suggests . . .

Carrying an onion in a pocket to ward off fits, wrapping dirty socks around the neck to drive away a sore throat, and treating freckles with stump water.

A sure cure for hiccups is one teaspoon of peanut butter, eaten all at once. Avoid leg cramps by turning shoes upside down before going to bed.

Cures for headaches include a flour sack tied over the head (better punch a hole in it for air), a wilted beet poultice on the forehead and, best yet, saving the clippings from your latest haircut and burying them under a rock.

Preventing nosebleeds can be accomplished in two ways—winding a piece of red woolen year around the neck and trimming nails only on Friday.

A potato carried in a pocket will absorb whatever causes rheumatism, axle grease is good for burns and garlic rubbed on bald heads will produce hair, as well as curing dandruff. Mother knew, by experience, that a flannel shirt soaked with lard and turpentine cured chest congestion.

This delightful entry concerning Fort Stanwix appears in the Gates Papers, in the New York Historical Society archives:

". . . has built a house by order of the general for one Stefanny who is married to a squaw 24 ft. long by 12 ft. wide."

THE HARVEST MOON

The Country Journal, that nostalgic magazine for those of us with farm upbringing, says the Harvest Moon is the time when it lights the early night landscape for a greater number of hours than at any other time of the year. On a clear night, at the designated time, the Harvest Moon provides full light from just after sunset to just before sunrise, being scientifically identified as the full moon closest to the Autumnal Equinox.

The Harvest Moon means more to us than the lyrics of that romantic song of our courtship days. We recall it fondly with remembrance of John T. McCutcheons' "Injun Summer" cartoon, first published in the *Chicago Tribune* in 1907.

It is magnificent, with a grandfather creating a glorious fantasy in graphic words, telling his little grandson that the leaves are red "about this time o' year" because when an "old Injun sperrit gets tired dancin'" it goes up "and squats on a leaf to rest" and that the leaves fall because "some fat old Injun ghost" gets too heavy.

The old man insists to his grandson that what he thinks is a cornfield, in the glow of the Harvest Moon, is not a cornfield but an Indian teepee village with redskins dancing in the mist. We grew up believing that the red in falling leaves came from the war paint that rubbed off the Indian spirits.

Brick Hasfield says an old-fashioned girl is one still married to her first husband.

DUTCH POTATO SALAD

A magazine piece sent us investigating both memory and one of Grandma's old cookbooks, the one of Holland Dutch influence.

There it was: German (Dutch) Potato Salad, something we knew about in childhood:

Half pound of bacon, fried crisp; a fine-chopped onion; six medium unpeeled potatoes; quarter teaspoon pepper; teaspoon salt; two tablespoons brown sugar; apple cider vinegar, as much as desired, a tablespoon at a time. Drain and crumble bacon; cube potatoes, skins and all; douse onion in bacon drippings; mix, season and stir. Serve warm, the vinegar making it "sweet and sour."

This is not new to lots of cooks. It just appeals to us as a childhood memory.

The mail contained a short note which stated: "I read your column every Friday and I'm going to keep on reading it until I like it."

Hyland Mills was called Parker's Mills, site of Parker Crystal Springs. Thomas R. Rees had a general store in Westernville. C. A. Nicholson operated the We-No-Ka greenhouses in Barneveld.

The Taberg Pump & Manufacturing Company was operating. Clark Briggs printed anything anyone wanted printed. Jerry Houser was postmsaster at West Branch.

The Rome *Sentinel* had a circulation of 8,000. You could get a room at the St. Charles Hotel at Sylvan Beach for $2.50.

In 1907!

FIRST TRAFFIC COP

The authorities of Rome were making a concerted effort to control motor traffic on downtown streets. Disturbed by the practice of automobiles to get through the business district at high speed—even up to 20 miles an hour—the police department was instructed to take action.

It responded by stationing a policeman at the Busy (American) Corner with instructions to watch for violators, be they drivers of cars and trucks or riders of bicycles.

The officer found this to be a difficult assignment. He had a common bicycle to chase the offenders and he reported he wasn't in necessary physical shape to catch up with youthful bicyclists.

The City Fathers responded to the crisis by providing the officer with a motorcycle, equipped with speedometer. This was in 1909.

Brick Hasfield says many a child is spoiled because its grandparents can't be spanked.

OUR FIRST CAR

We saw our first automobile sometime around 1914 when Mr. Johnson, a neighbor down the road from Dad's first farm, bought a Ford Runabout, a flashy black and red, open-seated, two-passenger vehicle.

The first car we drove was a new Star, an inexpensive automobile put out by William Crapo Durant, "grandfather" of General Motors, then operating on his own. This was in 1921, when our father scraped together a few hundred dollars to buy his first automobile. It also was the year Durant went bankrupt for the last time.

We had no driver's license. Nor did anyone else; it was not required. And we did not have parental permission to take the car for a ride. Our folks were away, the car was tempting, the starter plug was available. We backed it out of a shed and drove over to see our uncle, a couple of miles away. He advised us to get back home before our father arrived.

That we did. We didn't intend to knock part of the rear end of the shed down when we were unable to stop the car in time. What happened to us later is another story.

The first car we rode in was an early Austin-Healey; how Dad had it in 1919 we do not know. It had a red rubber top, anchored by leather straps running to the front fenders, straight out in the direction of travel above the tires. It was driven from the right side, shift lever outside the body of the car and had big, brass headlights lit by a match. The seats may have been of leather. It was a mystery car to us.

As we recall, the Star rattled a lot. The starter was activated by a notched steel plug which went into a hole in the dashboard.

Our very own first car was a one-of-a-kind sportster, developed from a 1919 Model T Ford, with underslung springs, custom-made two-seat wooden body and homemade convertible top, which never worked. We bought it in 1923 for $75. It was a classy rig; nothing like it. We sold it for $100. Our Lady refused to crank it any more and we needed the money. We drove it down Broadway once!

Then there was a 1921 Ford sedan, given to us by her father, which we ran only in the last half of the year. You could get a six-month license for $9 and few operated their cars in wintertime.

This was followed by the first car we bought as a family man, a 1921 Essex for which we paid $200 in 1930. It was the low-priced companion of the Hudson. Named after a place in England, the boxy Essex was the third largest selling car in 1929.

From then on, we've lost track of the succession of our automobiles over half a century—Ford, Buick, Reo, Chrysler products. We did not own a new car until immediately after World War II when we bought a Dodge sedan, for $1,950, we think. Because of shortages due to the war, its heater was not available for a year.

The Model T Fords were marvels, as everyone who had one knows. A novice could take the engine apart and put it back. Transmission bands were easy to install and adjust, even along the roadside. You could run out of gas on a hill, turn the car around and back up, reversing the gravity flow of the gasoline supply. If you were out of gas on the level and had someone to steer, standing behind the front seat, you could blow into the gasoline tank, beneath the driver's seat, and keep the engine running until you reached home or a service station.

What started this piece was a reference in *Cars & Parts* magazine of an automobile reportedly produced in Rome, New York, a French design built here under license around 1903—called the CGV, after Charon, Giradot and Voigt, whoever they were. We have always wondered if any Romans knew of Rome's CGV.

★   ★   ★

OLD DAYS IN ROME

Searching for some non-essential information, we happened to note a *Sentinel* classified ad of September 8, 1917, in which the Randolph Motor Company, 146 North Washington Street, offered taxi service with the stipulation: "No break-neck or night owl orders taken," whatever that might have meant.

The same paper said that the Home & Window Cleaning Company, 124 North Washington, would clean windows for 10 cents each. Other items reported that laborers were being paid 40 cents an hour, farmers were offered six cents a quart for their milk and that the community leaders were mobilizing to prevent termination of barge service to Rome on the Erie Canal.

And, most importantly, the *Sentinel* said the first draft contingent of World War I had departed for Fort Dix, New Jersey. Rome turned out with a parade and plenty of speeches to say "so-long for now" to Paul M. Schneible, Howard E. Carroll, Llewelyn E. Griffith, Eral C. Buyes, Jerry J. Gifford, Rudolph F. Burkard, John A. Henry and Willy S. Rudd of Rome; Edwin L. S. Smith, Yorkville; Charles Piete and Harry E. Foley, Whitesboro, and Hiram T. Baker and Fred Miller of Oriskany.

They were escorted to the railroad depot by a squad of the Rome Home Defense League, commanded by Sgt. Frank B. Williams.

Camden sent its first contingent that week: Leland C. Scoville, Theodore Pennington, Horace Johnson, Ferdinand Sutorius, Orville Manzer, Jr. and Lewis Burkett. The village turned out its home guard, 60 strong, and the Camden Military Band to escort the about-to-be soldiers to the station.

You are getting older if . . .

You remember how to get undressed in a Pullman upper berth. . . Your friends don't ask how you feel, but where you hurt. . . And many a day you feel like the morning after, but there wasn't a night before.

★   ★   ★

ROME THEATER HISTORY

Before the days of the Star, the Strand, the Family and the Capitol theaters, well remembered by those who go back to the 1920's, the folks in and around Rome went for amusement to the Casino, the Idle Hour, the Theatoriam, the Romahawk, Pells, the Family, Abbott's Opera House and Rome Opera House.

Reference files are blank, as far as we can ascertain, about these playhouses, except for the two well-known vacant stores turned into motion picture theaters—the Casino and the Idle Hour.

They opened when movies came to town, around 1910, admission five cents. The Casino, 135 North James Street, featured singer Bob Ward with Al Abrams at the piano. The Idle Hour, at 243-45 West Dominick Street, had similar programs. There is a picture of the four-person staff in the *Sentinel's* Rome Centennial edition of August 1, 1970—with no identification.

The Star, the Strand, the Family and the Capitol all ended their active days as operations of Kallet Theaters, Inc., Oneida, founded by Mike and Joe Kallet. In 1910, the brothers leased a vacant store in Onondaga Valley and started the first motion picture shows in that region. While Joe Kallet hand cranked the projector, Mike Kallet sought to lure patrons with a spiel outside on the sidewalk. First day receipts of less than one dollar did not discourage these young men who in a few years had movie houses in Camden, Hamilton, Baldwinsville, Canastota, Weedsport and Port Byron, not all at the same time.

Later they built the Madison Theater in Oneida and formed the Carroll Amusement Company which operated the Star and Strand in Rome. They erected the Capitol in 1928.

The Star had opened June 23, 1913, in a building at the corner of North James and East Willett Streets that had once been a livery stable. Purchased in 1922 by the Carroll Company, the Star operated until after the opening of the Capitol. The building, long a landmark, housed a Market Basket grocery store during World War II and is better known to some Romans as the Big Apple night club, starring Stella. It was demolished in the Urban Renewal program.

A new theater, in its own building, was established in 1913 by

J. H. Carroll, later a mayor of Rome. It was purchased in 1921 by the Carroll Amusement Company and renamed the Strand.

For a number of years, the Strand, then Rome's largest and best, offered silent movies and vaudeville. Stage shows were discontinued when the Capitol opened. Some may recall the local talent shows and boxing bouts on the stage.

The Strand was torn down some years before Urban Renewal, the theater having been closed for some time.

After the Capitol Theater had been dark for a number of years, it was "rescued" by a local group of enthusiasts who, against great odds and the expectations of some that their cause was hopeless, reopened the theater as the Capitol Civic Center.

Brick Hasfield says the man of the hour is the husband whose wife tells him to wait a minute.

AN AXE IN THE CAR

An axe was standard equipment in a car operated in Rome in the winters of the 1920's. It was common practice, as old-timers will attest, to "put the car up for the winter," placing the vehicle on blocks, taking off the tires and removing the battery to warm storage, covering the car with a large cloth or canvas. It stayed in the garage until spring. Those in winter service carried the axe.

The reason was simple. As much as four inches of snow might be left on the streets. They were not salted, thus providing good sleighing for those depending upon horses for winter travel.

That is, until there was a thaw, followed by a freeze, when streets became filled with icy ruts, inverted, confining tracks from which cars had difficulty leaving. Driving up to a corner, you could not turn the front wheels out of the ruts until you chopped switch outlets. When one met an oncoming car in the same ruts someone had to back up and get out of the track at the next intersection.

The *Sentinel* reported, in 1925, "sometimes these ruts get so deep that automobiles which get into them cannot get out. Some carry bags for such emergencies, bags of strong heavy material filled with sand. When the car is in the rut, the driver gets out and places one bag of sand in front of each front wheel. The car readily mounts the bags and front wheels may be turned out of the rut."

We drove cars in the winter and we read the *Sentinel*. We never used bags of sand; an axe was better. In fact, the bag method must have been for the upper crust.

Football season is the time of year when you can walk down the street with a girl on one arm and a blanket on the other—and no one says a word.

★   ★   ★

THE BIG STORMS

The statistics may be enlarged over the years, but all "worst storms" have validity. Ours include those of January 29-30, 1925 (our first winter in Rome) and January 23, 1936.

That storm of 1936 was a "doozy," riding out of the West on a sero-wind, high gales plugging roads with 10- and 12-foot drifts. Some Romans tunneled through sidewalk drifts rather than shovel a deep pass.

Trade was at a standstill, downtown was deserted. Funerals were postponed, doctors could not reach patients who, in turn, could not make it to a hospital. Streets and country roads were marked by snow-trapped vehicles. Sixty motorists were marooned for two days at the Fred Abbe home, near Oriskany Monument.

That blizzard lasted two days, but Rome was four getting back to normal. We find no mention in the *Sentinel* of total snowfall; all measurement concerned heights of drifts, 12 feet the unofficial record.

Later, on February 18, 1936, the Rome region was tied up for 18 hours—the same tale of blocked roads, stagnated business, stalled vehicles. Two days later, Verona was isolated for 48 hours. A steam shovel helped open the Rome-Westmoreland road. Lowell was not reached until February 25 when nearly 300 State School men and boys shoveled open the highway. Of some interest, they worked in a "heat wave," 33° above zero with dust storms blowing in from the West.

The year ended with the "worst April storm in decades," 60-mile winds, low temperatures and heavy snow.

March 25, 1940 found hundreds of cars stalled in drifts, many roads closed for four days, hundreds marooned. The same on March 19, 1941, stranded motorists in farmhouses, 20 sheltered in Stokes School House.

Our favorite great Rome storm? January 30, 1925. New to town, we awoke to four feet of snow, started walking at 7 a.m. for the job at Rome Wire, arrived between 9 and 10. Roads closed, even to horse traffic. Lake Shore Limited train stuck east of Rome depot. RW&O and Rome-Clinton lines blocked.

Sixty-five marooned in hall at Lowell; they danced until dawn. Mrs. Percy Hawkins, wife of the proprietor, served a hearty breakfast, pancakes, sausage, maple syrup and coffee.

And before the city was back to normal, the hollow stay bolt iron building of Rome Iron Mills, lower Canal Street, was destroyed in a $100,000 fire.

In 1925, the city did not have a fleet of snowplows. There were light blades on trucks and one 10-ton plow supported by the Rome Chamber of Commerce to keep roads open to nearby communities so people could shop in Rome.

Men long in the tooth have told of a crew from the State School shoveling a Rome & Clinton train out of drifts south of the school and we recall, date lost, when James Street was blocked for almost a week between present Walnut Street and Ridge Mills.

And we should not neglect the heavy persistent snows that blockaded railroad freight yards in World War II days of 1945, when Company D, 6th Regiment, New York Guard, shoveled snow for a week, in Rome and Utica.

It clings to memory because, not only did we think we were doing a public service, we were being paid as a first lieutenant, as a railroad track foreman, and bless its corporate heart, by our company. For which we slept in the old Armory, acted as mess officer for some 40 men and took turns with a shovel.

For folks of a more modern time, 1966 seems to be the "big storm." Strange that we do not remember much about it although we do know that George Waters, our publisher, read the comics over the *Sentinel* stations, WRUN and WRUN-FM, delivery of the paper to many subscribers being impossible.

Carl Windrath contributes these remembrances to our Memory File:

When the popular swimming pool in Rome was the Mohawk River at East Whitesboro Street, skinny dipping the practice. . . When there was an impromptu golf course from Canal Street to Lawrence to Louisa and back, five holes, dirt tees, fairways and greens. A second course, on East Wright Street, didn't open until after haying.

When there were 14 saloons from Ellinger's to the American Corner and a kid could make pocket money trapping muskrats along the Mohawk River and Wood Creek. . . When there was an ice rink on the site of Fort Stanwix School. . . And bicycle racks in front of stores and industrial plants. Around 1908.

★   ★   ★

A SPECIAL DAY

Anna G. Rosbrook, Rome superintendent of charities, reported spending $559.36 for "needed relief" to 148 individuals in 30 families in November of 1926.

The Dairymen's League announced it would pay a pool price of $2.72 per hundredweight for November milk. Milk was selling in stores for 13 cents a quart.

The Arcade Candy Shop in Rome was selling homemade ribbon candy for a quarter a pound, two pounds for 45 cents.

Spears Music House, 134 North James Street and Gurley Bros., 117 North Washington Street were advertising six-tube, one-dial Atwater Kent radios, with crook neck horns, price not revealed.

The Oneida County Board of Supervisors was considering the erection of a tuberculosis hospital on the Tanner farm, midway between Rome and Utica.

Coal was selling for $14.75 a ton and Woodruff Brothers, 118 Front Street, Rome, had new Chevrolet roadsters and touring cars for $510.

It was December 15, 1926 . . . the day we joined the *Sentinel* as an untrained reporter.

Brick Hasfield says about the time a fellow is cured of cursing, it's income tax time again.

YEAR OF GREAT RENOWN

If you remember . . . When the Boughton Drug Company store was in the Arlington Block; when F. E. Bacon Company advertised it was "Rome's greatest store"; when J. Karlen Cheese Company was at 513 West Court Street; when Jeremiah H. Carroll was mayor; when Joseph T. Owens was chief of police and George M. Bowers led the Fire Department; when Anna G. Rosbrook headed the Rome Bureau of Charities; when Charles T. Lanigan, Sr. was principal of Willett School; when Walter Davis ran the Rome-Westernville-Boonville stage; when W. Arthur Russ was president of the Rome Club; when A. R. Kessinger headed the Salmon River Fishing Club and H. D. Wolfe was president of Teugega Country Club; when Mrs. Edith Lee led the Women's Christian Temperance Union and when Rudd the Hatter was at 118 West Dominick Street . . . You were around Rome in the Fort Stanwix and Oriskany Sesquicentennial Year—1927!

Brick Hasfield says ideas are like children—your own are wonderful.

GREAT DAY OF 1927

It was August 6, 1927—the Sesquicentennial of the siege of Fort Stanwix and the battle of Oriskany.

Rome's greatest day in the lifetime of its proud citizens. They had been preparing for it for months. New streets and curbs were laid, at least half of the downtown buildings wore a new coat of paint, brick structures had been sand-blasted. Homes were repainted, lawns improved, walks and fences mended. The central business district was decked out in bunting and flags were flying all over the Flag City.

This observance, a major event in the statewide American Revolution Sesquicentennial, opened in Rome, August 3, with first-day issuance of the Burgoyne two-cent commemorative stamp, put on sale in Rome, Utica, Syracuse, Albany and Washington, D.C. There were ceremonies on the site of Fort Stanwix marking the 150th anniversary of the raising of the first Stars and Stripes in the face of the enemy.

The climactic day was Saturday, August 6. There were speeches in the morning at Oriskany battlefield, with presentation to the state of 4.87 acres of land, east of the ravine where the Patriots' column was ambushed, and dedication of the monument to the unknowns by the Oneida Historical Society, followed by the unveiling of tablets bearing 232 additional names of Herkimer's men, not listed on the original 1884 monument.

The day in Rome was built around Commander Richard E. Byrd and a two-and-a-half hour pageant at Mohawk Acres. Byrd had flown to the North Pole the year before and only the month previous across the Atlantic Ocean. He arrived early August 6 in a trimotor Ford Fokker plane, landing on a long, narrow meadow at the Donaldson farm at Cleveland Corners. This strip is now occupied by rear portions of depot buildings one, two and three at Griffiss AFB.

A cub reporter of seven months experience, this was our first major *Sentinel* assignment.

Six Army pursuit planes and three light bombers also landed here, to participate in fly-over demonstrations. One of the fighters made a safe emergency landing on the Craig farm, in the area of the present Rome Catholic High School.

The *Sentinel* headlined the Fort Stanwix-Oriskany pageant crowd as being around 100,000. Two days later, it hesitated, asking "how many stars are there in the heavens?" and quoting an unnamed "crowd expert" as estimating attendance at around 70,000.

The greatest crowd and the biggest traffic jam in Rome history began to develop around 11 a.m. After writing more than two columns about Byrd's arrival, we started for the pageant site, on the low land by the Mohawk River in the area now crossed by the Chestnut Street approach to the base. The crowd covered the high ground on two sides.

It took us 20 minutes to drive from the *Sentinel* office at 135 North James Street to Fort Stanwix Park and then it became apparent we would never reach Mohawk Acres to carry out our assignment of collecting crowd impressions. So we ran the car into the park and started walking. North James Street was so full of people, stalled in vehicles and crowding the sidewalks, that it took us nearly an hour to get to Mohawk Acres.

Directed by Nadine Currie, the pageant cast included many well-known citizens. That was the secret of the success of 1927. The committee simply told people what they were going to do and they did it. The pageant, with the Mohawk River and a one-third size wood and burlap replica of Fort Stanwix as backdrops, related familiar details of the siege. Donald White supervised building the "fort."

Commander Byrd and other dignitaries spoke and most of the crowd stayed in place for nearly four hours under a hot sun. A number of persons succumbed to the heat.

The great day closed with fireworks watched by more than 15,000 in the Vogel Park area of then unsettled upper North George Street. Many private parties, at local clubs and homes of the wealthy and not-so-wealthy took place that evening. Downtown was filled with people into the night; it took hundreds more than an hour to leave the pageant field.

The *Sentinel* published its now famous 102-page Sesquicentennial edition, containing the entire text of John A. Scott's "Fort Stanwix and Oriskany." The *Sentinel* editorial writer, our predecessor, wrote it and the newpaper company published it—in hard cover for $3.50—especially for the 150th anniversary. Today that hard cover is out of print and worth much more than the original price. Forty years after its publication, we paid $15 to a Canadian book dealer.

Albert R. Kessinger, editor and publisher of the *Sentinel*, a leader in the 150th observance and the man who secured passage of the 1935 Act of Congress that made possible Fort Stanwix National Monument, wrote in August of 1927:

"It is quite unlikely for decades to come—perhaps not until the 200th anniversary of the siege of Fort Stanwix and the battle of Oriskany—there will recur in this city a celebration having such a magnitude and significance."

The 200th anniversary, in 1977, was in no manner the great occasion of 50 years before, even if the Bicentennial observance was staged around the dedication of Fort Stanwix National Monument, culmination of a long community effort to mark Rome's significant American Revolutionary War history.

A grandfather knows that the trouble with giving the kids all those dance and music lessons is that you have to attend the recitals.

A GOLDEN YEAR IN ROME

The future of the city was bright . . . J.C. Penney had opened a new store at 221-225 West Dominick Street . . . J. Rosen had erected a new building for his store in the same block . . . the movers-and-shakers of the town were enthusiastic about a new community hotel—Gansevoort Inn—for which they had purchased land facing Gansevoort Park.

And Kallet Theaters, Inc.,—Myron Kallet of Oneida and Joseph Kallet of Rome—in conjunction with Commerford Amusement Company of Scranton, had opened, on December 10, 1928, the

2,500-seat Capitol Theater.

(The Stock Market crash which led to the Great Depression was a year away but there was no hint of the Dark Decade in 1928.)

Wages were not high by today's standards, but bread was only seven cents a loaf, pork loin a quarter a pound, sugar six cents, hamburger two pounds for 29 cents, sirloin steak 38 cents a pound and 15 pounds of potatoes 27 cents.

Then two years with the *Sentinel*, we were a $30-a-week reporter, unlimited hours, six days a week, no overtime, one week of vacation after two years—a great job for a young man who enjoyed his job with better than average pay at the time.

Those were optimistic days. The *Sentinel's* editorial on the opening of the Capitol declared: "With Gansevoort Inn to be built this spring, a new theater ready for dedication, several enlarged business blocks, a merger in the brass and copper industry that can only mean continued growth of local industries, almost definite assurance that a large chain store will locate here, Rome can look forward with confidence to a yearly increase in population."

Gansevoort Inn was never to be, the Depression choking off the mortgage market. But the Capitol, the finest theater for its size between Albany and Syracuse, continued to serve the community for 12,834 days, in good times and bad, until it went dark for movies May 29, 1974. In all that time, the Kallets never placed dollars above decency in the operation of that theater.

Today, the grand old theater is the Capitol Civic Center, rescued from oblivion and restored through the leadership of a young and enthusiastic group of citizens.

1928—The Good Year before Bad Times.

We were buying a doll for a little granddaughter when the saleslady said: "Here's a lovely doll. You lay her down and she closes her eyes and goes to sleep, just like a real little girl."

From experience, we realized that saleslady never had a real little girl.

GRIM DAYS OF THE 1930's

If you read the Rome *Sentinel* in 1933—in the early dark days of the Great Depression—you would have known that . . .

The Man-A-Block Plan was operating—a scheme where jobless men, sole supporters of a family, were provided some income by an arrangement whereby the "man on the block" shoveled or swept walks, carried ashes and trash from cellars to curb, and returned the receptacles, each participating family paying 50 cents a week, some of these families themselves living on $12 or less a week.

Gasoline was 17 cents a gallon, of which four cents were taxes—three for the state, one federal. Many persons could no longer afford to operate a car. Assemblyman Walter W. Abbott introduced a bill providing for a one-year moratorium on the sale of real property for unpaid taxes. Local traffic lights were set so that all turned green at the same time, to save gasoline.

New York farmers, who had been paid eight cents a quart for their milk in 1930, were getting less in 1933. Some went out of business.

Mayor W. B. Reid, M.D., was asked by the Common Council to bring about additional municipal pay cuts ranging from 10 to 35 per cent. He had already voluntarily secured a 10 per cent return from several city employees, including himself.

The Great Depression! Only old timers today know what it was like in the 1930's when one in every four persons able to work was without a job.

Brick Hasfield says a bartender is a psychiatrist with vertical patients.

A GLANCE AT 1934

Do citizens of Rome, New York, remember . . .

When Frank Krulinski made suits to order at 305 West Dominick Street? When the Dairymen's League had a plant at 221

South James Street? When a room could be rented for a dollar a night at the Arlington Hotel, corner of Dominick and Washington? When Spear's Music House sold Victrolas at 134 North James Street, next to the *Sentinel* office?

When Candyland (126 West Dominick Street) and Milvo's (149 North James Street) sold delicious homemade ice cream? When L. H. McCarthy sold Auburn, Cord, Dodge and Plymouth cars at 511 Arsenal Place?

When the Oneida County Savings Bank was at 178 West Dominick Street? When Charles T. Lanigan, Sr. was principal of DeWitt Clinton and Willett Schools? When the famous Rome Ale was produced by Rome Brewery, Inc., successor to Evans and Giehl, Inc., at 527 West Dominick Street?

When Rome had 34,496 inhabitants and Arthur C. Tedd was mayor?

If so, they were here in 1934.

Brick Hasfield says the problem with the new miracle medical treatments is that they may have side effects—like bankruptcy.

THE CIRCUS MADE HISTORY

The Ringling Brothers and Barnum and Bailey Combined Circus was "lost" in Rome early in July of 1935. Circus folks still talk about the Rome experience, when the big show, its grounds in Binghamton flooded, moved unexpectedly from Utica, at the close of a performance, to Rome—and attracted more than 10,000 persons with only a few hours notice.

It was the time of the Great Flood of the Southern Tier. The circus had played in Schenectady July 9, moved to Utica for the 10th and was billed for Binghamton for the 11th. But that date was suddenly stricken from the schedule, a cancellation that led to unprecedented events in circus history. Not only was the Binghamton lot under water, railroads to that city were out of service.

Early in the morning of July 10, 1935, Sam Gumpertz, the circus general manager, made a bold decision. The show would move, with its four trains of 100 railroad cars, 14 miles to Rome where it would unload, feed its stock and give the usual two performances on the 11th, without the customary advance advertising.

The 33,000 people of the City of Rome, and those in the Rome area, had no idea the circus was coming. There was only one day to announce the unexpected event and to create anticipation among the populace.

Roland Butler, the advance man, was at first against the plan. He had no playbills up, no ads running, none of the usual publicity. His boss was adamant, "We play in Rome in 36 hours."

Butler, a pro in press relations, said he knew there was only one way to reach most of the people with impact—the town's newspaper! He phoned Everiss Kessinger, *Sentinel* managing editor, in the middle of the night, ordering a two-page ad for July 10. There was no time to discuss ad rates, no time to sign contracts, put up broadsides, do any of the usual promotion.

Mayor Arthur C. Tedd issued the necessary permit—no papers signed—and helped secure the lot, where two years before the Hagenback & Wallace Circus had appeared. The New York Central Railroad began clearing unloading tracks in the Rome yard, near the Spargo Wire Company, off South Madison Street.

What may have geen the largest circus newspaper ad—two facing pages—appeared in the *Sentinel* of July 10, 1935:

LIKE A THUNDERBOLT OUT OF A CLEAR SKY!
RINGLING BROS. AND BARNUM & BAILEY
COMBINED CIRCUS AT ROME
TOMORROW, THURSDAY, JULY 11 at 2 & 9 P.M.

"Owing to the Quickest Change in Route in the History of Gigantic Amusements, Due to the Disastrous Flood Conditions in the Empire State's Southern Tier, the Greatest Show on Earth, ALL IN ITS VAST ENTIRETY, Will Bring to Rome the Most Colossal Aggregation of Marvels in the History of the World."

A "double truck"—two full pages—with headlines in 140-point wooden "buckshot" type. The front page headline declared "Ringling Bros. Barnum & Bailey's Combined Circus Coming to

Rome, Thursday, July 11." A big story on page two reported the circumstances, plus pictures of circus stars on several pages.

And that's not all on the part of the *Sentinel*. That issue was distributed that day to every place in the *Sentinel* area, subscribers and non-subscribers. We know; we helped deliver throughout the countryside.

We do not recall the price of admission. It was not mentioned in ads or news and it did not matter to us. We had a pocket full of passes. So did everyone at the *Sentinel*.

It was a thrilling sight about 6 in the morning of the 11th to see a big herd of elephants marching up Madison Street to the lot between Madison and James, past Chestnut, in those days not yet developed.

It took six hours for the circus to unload and move to the show grounds, its wagons and animals clogging two routes, East Dominick and North James, and South and North Madison. By 10:30 a.m., hundreds of spectators were at the circus grounds watching the 16,000-seat Big Top go up.

The circus did more business that unannounced day then any circus that had ever played in Rome. Butler, a pro in the business, declared, "This is the initial instance when the power of newspaper advertising, with no other medium included, was ever tried out on a circus. And it worked!"

It was a unique day for the circus personnel. The circus was literally "lost," no communication with the advance billing staff, no mail waiting at the post office.

All of the 31 circus tents, seven herds of elephants, 1,009 other animals, and 1,600 people (circus figures) were on the James-George-Madison grounds by noon, preparing for the 2 p.m. show.

We interviewed Col. Tim McCoy, Western movie star of those days, who headed "The Congress of Rough Riders," the main attraction of the "After Show." He had been visiting Rome friends, among them James Maloney, Thomas J. Connell, James D. Casey and Francis Finley.

Only one accident was reported. A circus draft horse had to be destroyed after it fell and broke an ankle.

What a day! We remember it well, especially for a personal reason. With our flock of passes, we took friends and neighbors to the evening performance, posturing as a "big shot" with box seats in the very front by the center ring.

In those days we smoked cigars—a lot of them—and had an unlighted one in our mouth, a vulgar exhibition, our Lady said then and says now. A clown was tossing a large rubber ball at the rear end of a donkey, the animal unerringly kicking the ball into the audience.

We turned from talking with someone just as the big ball hit us square in the face. The cigar vanished down our throat and, we still insist, "we darn near died."

The crowd laughed. Those who remember still think it was part of the act.

The circus left in the morning hours of the 12th, leaving its unique addition to Rome history.

Brick Hasfield says never lend money to a fellow who boasts of having six credit cards.

GANSEVOORT'S UNIFORMS

We had a connection with the securing of pictures of the uniform Col. Peter Gansevoort wore at Fort Stanwix, when at the age of 28 he commanded the garrison that turned back the British invasion of the upper Mohawk Valley.

We were at a meeting of The Company of Military Historians in Washington when, at a reception in the Armory Hall of the Smithsonian, Our Lady suggested we view a figure on a mannequin, "near the tent of General Washington." The uniform was identified as that of Col. Gansevoort in 1777 at Fort Stanwix, presented to the Smithsonian by his great-granddaughter, Catherine Gansevoort Lansing of Albany. She gave the Gansevoort Statue in Gansevoort Park, Rome.

In Washington's tent was the field bed used by Gansevoort at Fort Stanwix and, off to a side, on another mannequin was Gansevoort's uniform as a brigadier general of the regular army at the start of the War of 1812. He died that year without seeing active service.

The story behind all this involves Congressman Alexander Pirnie whose help we sought in securing the photographs. About six weeks later, again in Washington, we visited Armory Hall and found a camera crew of six, with backdrops, step ladders, lights and several cameras, clustered around the model of young Gansevoort. When we asked what was going on, the fellow who seemed to be in charge, said:

"Oh, some editor in the country wants pictures of that guy in the old uniform."

We did not identify ourselves.

Brick Hasfield says no nation should go to war until it has paid for its last one.

DEERSLAYER RESTS IN AVA?

Is the original of Hawkeye (Natty Bumpo) buried on a knoll at Ava? Is Nathaniel Foster, Jr. the prototype of James Fennimore Cooper's *Deerslayer, Pathfinder, Leatherstocking*?

When the old woodsman's grave was marked in June of 1937 on the Traxel farm at Ava, the tradition sprang to life again, to contend with claims that Cooper's hero was fashioned after men of old in Hoosick Falls, Cooperstown or in Onondaga County.

Nat Foster, born in 1776, died March 16, 1840 at the home of his daughter, Jermima Edgerton, in an old stone house at Ava, on what was known, in 1937, as the Harrington farm.

He never claimed to be Cooper's image for Hawkeye, the white scout of *The Last of the Mohicans*. Cooper knew Foster well, but said his character could have been fashioned after several men. Folks at Hoosick Falls declared Nathaniel Shipman was Bumpo and erected a statue to him in 1915.

Historically inclined residents of Cooperstown said Shipman's brother, David, was the man pictured by Cooper. Onondaga's contender was Ephriam Webster, a pioneer settler.

The Rev. A. L. Bryon-Curtis, at one time of Rome, in his 1897 book, *The Life and Adventures of Nat Foster, Trapper and Hunter of the Adirondacks*, flatly declared that Foster was Cooper's Leatherstocking character. So said Judge Hurlbut, who defended Foster at his trial for killing an Indian at Old Forge.

J. P. Edgerton, great-grandson of Nat Foster, led the movement to erect the 1937 gravestone at Ava. He was assisted by Ernest Countryman whose grandfather had told him Foster was Natty Bumpo.

Countryman wrote: "There are two mounds in the old orchard-cemetery (at Ava), side by side. One is that of Natty Bumpo and the other is that of the village founder, but even the oldest inhabitant has forgotten which is 'tother. It shouldn't be difficult to find out for certain as the ground is sandy and dry and Natty had all double joints."

Later, it was decided that the Foster grave is the closest to the Ava-Point Rock road. The old cemetery, once believed to hold the remains of some 60 persons, is in a meadow about an eighth of a mile from Ava Corners. Many years ago the cemetery was reduced in size when, year after year, plows encroached and markers disappeared.

Nat Foster was a legend of the early 1880's, an expert in loading and firing muzzle-loading guns. He would wager that he could fire his musket six times in a minute. And genereally win, the story goes. Four shots was fast time. Foster had a habit of carrying his musket balls between his fingers, to save time.

He was reputed to have killed several Indians, but was brought to trial only once, on a charge of murdering Peter Waters, commonly called Druid, an Indian enemy, at Indian Point, near Old Forge. In the trial, at Herkimer, a jury presided over by Judge Hiram Denio of Rome, found Foster not guilty, evidence being that Druid had tried to ambush Porter.

Cooper, a son of the pioneer and wealthy family that settled Cooperstown soon after the Revolution, wrote a novel on English life which was not well received and then, as a success, a story of a spy in Westchester County during the war with Britain. That was well acclaimed.

Cooper made Natty Bumpo famous in the *The Last of the Mohicans*, written in 1826. Later he brought the scout back to literary life in 1840 in *The Pathfinder*, following the next year with *The Deerslayer*.

It really doesn't matter whether Natty Bumpo was written after Nat Foster. Cooper's Leatherstocking tales may be more enjoyable if the reader goes along with the legend that the prototype of a famous literary hero rests in an obscure grave at Ava. It might even make Cooper's stilted, difficult to stay with, writings more enjoyable.

Brick Hasfield says politicians and cars are both subject to recalls.

BILL MAXHAM'S TREE

Many old-timers point out landmarks of their life, where they once lived, went to school and such. We have a special interest in a living reminder of an episode in a long existence—a hearty tree at the northwest corner of James and Linden Streets, the one behind the mail drop box.

It stands today with a trunk at least 12 inches in diameter. When we ran over it, in a Model-T Ford, it had been there a couple of years. It bent, but as present condition proves, it did not break. It is more than 60 years older now.

Let the record show that we were not driving. With Our Lady we were returning from a long, two-blowout trip with our father-in-law, who must have been inattentive, weary or distracted.

Whatever, he drove up North James Street and made a wide left turn for the 100 block of West Linden Street, swinging out over the sidewalk and directly over the young sapling, which quickly sprang back, with only a small part of bark disturbed.

He said nothing, driving on to his 123 West Linden Street home as if nothing of note had happened. He's been gone since the 40's, a good man, fun to be with once one understood him and his straight arrow upbringing, but not the best driver we have known.

For us and his daughter, it's the William H. Maxham Tree.

Brick Hasfield says there comes a time when the Happy Hour becomes a nap.

Once upon a time . . .

Thornton W. Burgess told Bedtime Stories and Dr. Brady gave health advice in the *Sentinel*. J. Rosen sold Florsheim shoes for $7.65 a pair at 268 West Dominick Street. The best movies of the year were "Mutiny on the Bounty," "Dr. Deeds Goes to Town" and "The Great Ziegfeld," in that order.

Emily F.F. Halstead operated a travel agency at 506 North Madison Street. Amos n' Andy, The Hit Parade, Uncle Ezra, Boake Carter, Burns and Allen, Benny Goodman, Lowell Thomas, Easy Aces and Lum and Abner were hits on the radio. The *Sentinel* comic strips were Joe Palooka, Dixie Dugan, Mickey Finn, Scorchy Smith, The Phantom, Skippy and Cap Stubbs.

Ray Heath's bright and homey columns in the *Sentinel* were the best of their kind in the state.

Porterhouse steak was 32 cents a pound, hamburg two pounds for a quarter at the Mohican grocery on East Dominick Street.

In the 1937 days of the Great Depression.

A fellow walked into a florist shop and said: "I need something to go with a weak alibi."

LOOK BACK IN YEARS

Can you guess the year . . .

When adult admission to R.F.A. football games was 50 cents, if purchased in advance? When range oil was selling for 8½ cents? When the Dionne Quintuplets were featured in the movie "Five of a Kind" at the Capitol Theater?

When the Ladies Aid Society of the Ava Methodist Episcopal Church was serving an oyster supper for 35 cents? When Uvanni's Restaurant and the Eagle Restaurant were advertising spaghetti dinners, with hot sausage and peppers, for 15 cents?

When the *Sentinel* reported that "frocks are smart and coats distinctive, but it's the nonsense on heads and hands that puts charm on the wearer, and muffs are popular with gloves that give them color?"

And when Jack Dempsey, in Rome campaigning for Governor Lehman's re-election, was greeted by a crowd of 5,000 in front of Stanwix Hall? In November, 1938.

Despite the high price of whiskey, a 25-cent drink is still available in some of the Appalachian mountain regions—a recent autopsy has revealed.

RADAR AND TEDDY JR.

We were covering First Army maneuvers in the Ogdensburg region in 1940, driving alone on a back road when we were hailed by a lone officer, a colonel or brigadier, we have forgotten. He raised his walking stick and asked for a ride, saying his jeep had broken down and his driver had gone for assistance.

As we drove on our way back to headquarters we saw several tents in a cluster in a nearby field, with a curious array of what we thought were radio antennas. The officer suggested we stop and take a look. When we observed that a sign said, "Off Limits," he ignored us and commanded, "come along." Stopped by a sentry, he soon was passed on, we close behind.

The main tent was filled with strange equipment, some of it looking like small mirrors. As we left and were driving along, the officer introduced himself as Theodore Roosevelt and quietly remarked that we would be hearing more about what we had seen but perhaps we had better not talk about it.

Did Theodore Roosevelt, Jr. expose us to our first glimpse of early radar? We've always thought so.

He died, an assistant divisional commander, in Normandy shortly after D-Day. He had been warned about a heart condition, but who was going to send back the son of a president on such a day? The movie, "The Longest Day," shows Henry Fonda, playing Teddy Roosevelt, Jr., gathering scattered troops on the beach and, walking stick pointing the way, leading them into action, heart problems ignored.

Brick Hasfield says the average fellow makes sure his car is working, whether he is or not.

WHEN THE AIR DEPOT CAME

Griffiss AFB, activated February 2, 1942, has been close to us since April 4, 1941, when two U.S. Army officers came to Rome seeking a possible location for something they called an "air depot."

After these many years, we think it best to make this confession: We knew for certain that Rome was going to be the site of the air depot a month before the Army's announcement. And so did several other Rome-Utica citizens, all of us keeping the secret because of fear that premature disclosure might jeopardize the project.

Here's how it happened:

There was great uncertainty about the location of the great prize —a $14 million facility employing 2,000 persons, it was indicated.

Baldwinsville, Binghamton and a site on the north shore of Oneida Lake were prominently mentioned by Army sources. We know now they were seeking to divert our attention.

A Rome-Utica delegation went to Washington, ostensibly as delegates to the annual meeting of the U.S. Chamber of Commerce. It included Gordon E. Kent, Goerge H. Barrows, James C. O'Shea and Fritz S. Updike of Rome, Charles S. Donnelley, James G. Capps and George Winslow of Utica.

The delegation ignored the Chamber sessions to call on its national legislators. Senators Meade and Lehman could provide no definite information. Congressman Merritt, an at-large House member from New York, was elusive.

As the delegation left his office, Barrows, formerly on the staff of the *Washington Post*, said: "Merritt is on the House Armed Forces Committee; he knows. We'll find out tonight."

Tonight meant the New York State Chamber of Commerce cocktail party at the Mayflower Hotel. When the local delegation assembled for the state affair, Burrows appeared with two attractive women. He quickly issued instructions: "When Merritt shows up, introduce the girls and disappear."

We were at the bar when someone tapped us on the shoulder and asked, in a familiar voice, "Why don't you fire and fall back?" There was the Congressman. We quickly introduced him to the ladies—and vanished. A short time later one found several of us talking in a corner and quietly said: "Rome is getting the air depot."

Not much later, Congressman Merritt asked Gordon Kent, president of the Rome Chamber, to assemble our delegation. He did, in a vacant room off to one side of the cocktail party.

Merritt confirmed that the air depot was coming to Rome but added: "I've been talking too much and I want you to know this. If this gets out, the decision could be changed." He went on to say there was heavy political pressure from other areas and repeatedly warned that we could blow the whole thing.

So we returned home and wrote around the story, hinting at a great economic expansion and, repeatedly, of the vital need for more housing—quick!

Everyone kept the faith, as far as we know, and it was not until

May 21, 1941, that the War Department unofficially hinted that the decision had been made and not until June 25th of that year did the official word come down through political channels.

Oh, about those who charmed the Congressman. All was on the straight and narrow as far as the local delegation was concerned— Gordon Kent, noted for morality and dignity, was our chaperone.

Brick Hasfield says that if you wonder what a woman sees in a man it's probably a reconstruction job.

WAR RATIONING DAYS

An old friend, now gone on ahead, had one of the most thankless jobs on the home front in World War II. Maurice G. Steele was chairman of the Rome Price and Ration Board from November 1942 to January 1945.

This volunteer agency—only the small staff was paid—began soon after Pearl Harbor, being appointed under federal regulations by then Rome Mayor Walter W. Abbott, John H. Reifert was the first chairman, with ex-Mayor Arthur C. Tedd and Steele and other members. Steele succeeded Reifert and stuck to the onerous job until the last year of the war.

In addition to gas rationing, the board had control of fuel oil, meats, boots and shoes, some foodstuffs, automobiles, bicycles and a long list of essentials. Clarence Peacock headed the staff, Frances Powers was secretary.

It was not a popularity contest for any of those involved. They were the targets of much grumbling by the public and often sharp personal criticism. On the whole, however, there was patriotic compliance by the majority of the people.

Nevertheless, one old man, who had been refused stamps for a new pair of rubber boots, took his manure-covered old boots off in the Rome office and, tossing them high in the air, shouted: "Take 'em! You need 'em more than I do!"

A regional Office of Price Administration office in Syracuse investigated numerous violations, most of them settled without publicity. Old timers will recall persistent rumors of black marketing, particularly in gasoline for which extra ration stamps generally were available, or gasoline secured without such authorization.

It was estimated by officials who should have known that about 20 percent of the meat supply moved through illegal channels and that the gasoline violations were extensive.

World War II gas rationing was based on a basic A-book which produced about 3.6 gallons a week. Persons who proved additional need could obtain B and C stamps for extra supplies. The OPA said rationing reduced gasoline usage about 420 million gallons daily.

There were red stamps for meat, butter, fats, cheese, canned milk and canned fish. Blue stamps covered fruits and vegetables. Cigarettes were not rationed but were often scarce, the troops in the field having first priority.

A certificate from the ration board was necessary to buy an automobile or truck tire or to have a used one recapped. For a time during the war you couldn't legally buy or have a pair of shoes retapped without authorization. Sugar rationing began in May of 1942 and was not lifted until June of 1947, months after the end of the war.

Clothing, aside from shoes, was never rationed but some lines became scarce when the GIs came streaming home to get out of uniform. There were unrationed shoes on the market but it was best not to walk with them in the rain. You might lose the paper soles.

Those of us who lived through World War II rationing knew that it was better to take a wife or girl friend a steak than a bunch of flowers.

Brick Hasfield says the best diet forbids eating between snacks.

HARD TIMES

Notes from an almost forgotten speech we made about hard times Old Timers will remember . . .

Rome, like all America, was wallowing in deep depression when Franklin D. Roosevelt became the 32nd president of this nation. "If I fail," he said, "I shall be the last."

All four Rome banks, Rome Trust Company, Farmers National Bank and Trust Company, Rome Savings Bank and Oneida County Savings Bank, were closed when he took the oath of office. So were many in the country. Within hours he shut all the banks. Many of them, including Rome's, reopened for limited business March 7. You could open new accounts and draw on them but you could not take out funds from old ones.

FDR took office declaring "the only thing we have to fear is fear itself." President Hoover had said the "country is on the verge of financial panic and chaos." He seemed incapable of effective action; he and FDR could not, or would not, agree on emergency measures. The United States was technically bankrupt.

The publisher of the *Sentinel*, A. R. Kessinger, kept $20 for office change and split the rest of the money in the till among his employees, each getting $2.35. Our Young Lady had less than $5 at home. A good Samaritan, C. F. W. Trabant, local insurance agent, met us on the street and without solicitation gave us $10, saying, "Pay it back when things settle down." We breezed through the bank holiday.

At that time, 1,400 Rome men were reporting daily for jobs on "home relief," only 200 being hired, on a rotating basis, for odd jobs. Two thousand five hundred Romans were receiving "home relief," then the words for "welfare." Public assistance wasn't much in those days.

Revere stock was selling for $1.50 a share. Those with faith in Rome's biggest industry made money. General Motors was under $10 a share, you could see Mae West at the Capitol Theater for 25 cents and buy a roast beef dinner for 35. Sirloin steak was 23 cents a pound, coffee a pound for a quarter, hamburger three pounds for 25 cents. (After Roosevelt's first week or so, the price went to two pounds for a quarter, the "hamburger pool of confidence," some fellow said.)

Eggs had been as low as 12 cents a dozen, at the farm. Dairymen were getting less than a dollar a hundred for their milk, at the lowest point. Stock prices were now 11 per cent of their 1929 values.

Roosevelt called the Congress back and within a week or so, often with the Congressional bills as yet unprinted, ordered emergency action. Stock prices jumped 15 per cent. All "solid" banks had reopened by March 15. Nearly 5,000 of them had gone out of buisness.

In 10 days, Congress passed legislation that changed the course of the nation, the beginning of the New Deal—Civilian Conservation Corps, Tennessee Valley Authority, National Recovery Act, relief for farmers, for the poor and homeless, emergency job programs. It was a political honeymoon never seen since.

One had to go through it to know what it was like—days when the only money you had was in your pocket, bread lines growing longer in big cities, the government impotent and then—a great burst of national faith and pride in a man in the White House who acted. Correctly or incorrectly, he acted.

Will Rogers put it well: "We had no jobs, we had no money, and if Roosevelt had burned down the Capitol, we would have said, 'Thank God, he started a fire under something.'"

Back in the days when we were active in the newspaper profession, the phone by our bed rang at 3 one morning. An elderly feminine voice asked: "Are you the editor of the *Sentinel*?"

We replied that we were and asked what we could do for her at that time of morning. "Well," she said, "I'm an old lady and I do not sleep well. When I am awake I read. I am reading your paper and every other page is blank."

We responded that if she would give us her address we would get a complete paper for her in the morning. "But you don't understand," she replied. "I like the *Sentinel* better this way."

D-DAY IN ROME

The Capitol Theater in Rome was playing a double bill—Hedy Lamar and William Powell in "The Heavenly Body" and Erich Von Stroheim, Vera Rolston and Richard Arlen in "The Lady and the Monster . . ."

Rome Manufacturing Minstrels were about to entertain at the RFA Alumni Reunion . . ." Westmoreland Grange was advertising a 5-cent supper . . ."

Sam's Pant Shop offered boys' gabardine trousers "just like Dad's" for $4.95 . . ." New Riverdale Village was renting new 4½-room bungalows for $40 a month . . ."

Birds Eye Snyder Division of General Foods was desperately advertising for help—"work as little as 4 hours per day, at highest prevailing wages . . . with associates of highest calibre, civic leaders, business and professional men, housewives and other good Americans"—at 128 East Garden Street . . ."

Automobile use stamps - $5 - were on sale at the Internal Revenue office at the Post Office . . ." General Motors stock was selling at 61, Hudson Motors 12½, General Electric 36, AT&T 160½ and New York Central 46 . . .

The Rome *Sentinel* began posting window bulletins at 2:15 a.m. and published its first edition at 10:05 a.m. It was June 6, 1944—D-Day!

★ ★ ★

A DAY TO REMEMBER

Some folks say they like these old-time guessing games, so here goes:

Sirloin steak was selling for 29 cents a pound, potatoes 39 cents for 15 pounds, bananas four pounds for a quarter, at Market Basket stores. Victory had flour at 73 cents for 24½ pounds, coffee 21 cents a pound sack.

The Rome Colonels of the Canadian-American Class C League had won the season's opener, 12 to 6, over Utica with 1,189 in the local park on Black River Boulevard. Rome players included Berger, Eremisch, Hill, Riley (the manager), Bloch, Miller, Kam,

Clifton, Crockett, Case, Elsie, Young, Molinelli and Gorman.

Keller's sold dresses at 246 West Dominick; the Allen Shop, 183 West Dominick, was advertising fine needle-points. Ed Maxwell had a 1939 Ford sedan on sale for $475.

Chauncey S. Beckwith was selling insurance for C. Mark McLaughlin. Rome Cable Corp. had boosted the pay of all earning less than $250 a month by 10 per cent.

The Camden Philharmonic Club had completed 52 years of activities. W. Fred Pepper, owner of the fishing tackle business bearing his name, had retired after 50 years, dating back to the day when his father, John Pepper, Sr., had bought out his partners, P. H. Hook and John B. MacHarg, in the firm started in 1891.

Rome's Methodist preachers, Dr. A. C. Goddard, pastor First Methodist Church since 1936, and the Rev. H. D. Holmes, at Calvary Methodist, had been returned by the Conference.

Joseph O'Brien, Sr. celebrated his 81st birthday. Rome's No. 1 baseball fan had been proprietor of the famed Empire House, adjacent to the site of the southwest bastion of Fort Stanwix, for 41 years.

Rome milk dealers were appealing for the prompt return of empty milk bottles. The Rome Community Chest had made its goal, raising $4,185 more than its quota of $61,562. Ken Bow was president, Ross Fraser campaign chairman.

C. Judd Feickert of VanHornesville had been appointed director of music in Rome public schools.

Gibson electric refrigerators were selling for $94.50 at the new G&F Electric Company, 138 East Dominick Street, owned and operated by A. Giordano and R. Ferlo. June's Bakery, on West Court Street, was selling bread for 12 cents a loaf.

The Rome Board of Education had authorized purchase of six acres of land for $10,000 and acceptance of an option to buy, for $25,000, the balance of the George W. Lane property, including buildings, adjacent to Rome Free Academy, on Turin Street. These 15 acres were required for athletic facilties.

All this within a week of April 4, 1941—when four Army officers came to Rome looking for a site for something called an Air Depot.

★ ★ ★

BREAKFAST WITH PATTON

We celebrated a national holiday at breakfast with General George S. Patton, Jr., years ago in a South Carolina forest, theoretically a "prisoner of war."

It was in late November and we were a "war correspondent" attached to the First (Blue) Army, in maneuvers against the Fourth (Red) Corps, with 220,000 troops involved in a three-state area. Serious business, too, 93 soldiers dying in the exercise, 80 in accidents, 13 from natural causes.

With Harold Martin, Atlanta columnist who became a star war correspondent in Europe for the *Saturday Evening Post*, we were driving along between Cheraw and McBee, South Carolina, when Martin said: "Let's go see General Patton."

Totally bewildered, we said: "Patton? He's the enemy, he has the Fourth Tank Corps. He's the Red commander. We are Blues. And we don't know where Patton is."

"So what," said Martin, "we'll get captured." And we did.

Driving down a rural road, with a blue banner flying on the *Sentinel* car, we were stopped by a Red patrol, the lieutenant of which didn't know what to do with us. He didn't know where Patton was, he hadn't been told about prisoners.

Martin kept saying, "We are newspaper correspondents. We want to see General Patton." "Well, I don't," said the lieutenant. "He's tough."

He sent us, under a one-man guard, to his company commander, down the road several miles, who shrugged his shoulders and sent us on, now with three escorts, to the headquarters of a Georgia regiment. We were lucky to be in the hands of Georgians.

Martin quickly establishing an "at home" relationship with the G-2 (intelligence) officer who allowed that perhaps Patton might like to see news people but he would have to check. After lunch in the field (yes, dried beef on bread), the major took us and another lieutenant over back country dirt roads, maybe eight miles, to a lightly wooded area near Pageland, South Carolina, in which trailers, trucks and tents were parked—Patton's headquarters.

The major was chewed out by the intelligence officer of the 4th Corps for creating an unusual problem but, again, Martin found a fellow newspaperman, a lieutenant colonel serving reserve time on Patton's staff, handling press relations. We were lucky.

Both officers said they didn't know how the general would react and that we were to spend the night at headquarters, as prisoners. "God help you," the G-2 officer said, "if you turn out to be Blue infiltrators."

After a piece of meat and bread for supper, and a shot of whiskey from the newspaper officer, we were ordered to turn in on strung litters in an ambulance, two privates from New Orleans guarding us, in their sleep on the floor beneath. Before they started snoring, Martin had led them in a descriptive tour of the attractions in the famous Latin Quarter of that Louisiana city.

Came morning and we prepared for what might be ahead, not knowing what it would be. Suddenly, General Patton, pearl-handled pistols in holsters on each side of calvary trousers, with a short, trim jacket and a soft cap with two stars, came striding out of a tent and over to us. He stuck a riding crop into our stomach and demanded: "What the hell are you damned Blues doing here?"

When we tried to explain our desire, as correspondents, to talk with him, he said he was going to send us through prisoner-of-war exchange which was looking for "raw bait to work on."

Then he smiled and invited us to a table of pancakes, ham, biscuits and coffee, and started to talk, ignoring all questions. He deplored the shortages of equipment in his command, particularly trucks and tanks, said his armored vehicles were fit only for training, wouldn't last long against the Germans, and declared (we remember his words well), "this country has to know what it faces and you two can help by writing the truth."

Continuing in this theme, he spoke, and sharply, for several minutes, then asked if we wanted to try the prisoner-exchange route back home. In desperation, we told him we had to be in Richmond, Virginia, the next day, to meet our wife who was coming down to drive home with us. That wasn't the truth but it was the best we could do. (After all, prisoners of war were supposed to give only name, rank and serial number.)

General Patton walked away, turned and strode back to us. He asked if we wanted to see some excitement and if we'd do our best with it and, without waiting for an answer, told us to be at a certain road junction at 10 a.m. "Don't sit around as if you own the place," he warned. "And you never saw us, remember!"

We thanked him and his staff for an unusual occasion, found the intersection of two dirt roads in time and a Blue infantry regiment lolling around, officers consulting maps and with no time for "reporters playing war correspondents." Then, from a hedgerow about half a mile across a sandy field, came a column of Red tanks—Patton!

After a brief fire fight, with blanks, the umpires declared the Blue force had been driven back two miles. We started north for press headquarters, a long way off at Southern Pines, and driving up to an aged white building at a crossroad, we noted the sign: "White Store." That spot is so designated on South Carolina maps today.

As we nibbled at crackers and cheese, Martin asked with a grin: "My Yankee friend, what day is this?"

He answered his own question: "Thanksgiving."

Neither of us knew it was 15 days to Pearl Harbor!

Brick Hasfield says one of the worst things about retirement is having to drink coffee on your own time.

RADC AND POLITICS

Those who do not believe that political pressures can influence military decisions should research the history of Rome Air Development Center (RADC) at Griffiss AFB.

RADC is and always has been most important to the vitality of the Rome base. Creation of the RADC plan—centralization of air electronics at Griffiss—prevented deactivation of Rome Army Air Field after World War II. It saved the base, secheduled in 1947 to gradually shut down, its wartime need at an end. That order was revoked in 1948 when the RADC plan came into being.

In the original RADC proposal Rome was to have become a prime center of Air Force electronics. Watson Laboratories, at Red Bank, New Jersey; Cambridge Laboratories, near Boston; and Wright-Patterson Field, Ohio, electronic activities were to have been centralized at what is now Griffiss AFB.

This did not happen, mainly because of political pressures by the localities involved and opposition in the scientific community. Only a small visual display laboratory came from Cambridge, whose staff was successful in having a prestigious national scientific committee appointed to survey the consolidation proposal. It recommended rejection. The few civilian scientists already in Rome remained. Only a part of the Wright-Patterson activities came to Rome.

Watson Laboratories is a fascinating story of politics, on both sides of the proposition. Whether the New Jersey people would move to Rome became the center of a prolonged political struggle.

The opposition might have been softened if the Oneida-Oswego congressional district had not gone Democratic in 1948 by less than 500 votes. This district had been a safe Republican seat for years. Congressman Hadwen Fuller of Pulaski was considered certain of re-election.

It was 1948; President Truman, running for election in his own right, was most unpopular, even the experts agreed. Local Democrats had difficulty finding a candidate to oppose Fuller and finally decided that their public relations expert, young Jack Davies, scion on a one-time leading Republican family, would make the sacrifice.

Harry Truman was elected, in an astonishing victory, and carried Davies into Congress by a relatively handful of votes. When the Air Force construction bill came up in the House Armed Services Committee, with some $3 million for RADC in Rome, the bill was defeated, the deciding vote cast by a New York Republican, all GOP members rallying to the support of Republican New Jersey, home of Watson.

The struggle of the GOP to keep Watson Labs in New Jersey became deeply involved in party maneuvers. Both national committees took a hand in the tug-of-war over what was, in terms of money, a small item in the construction authorization bill.

The RADC item, authorizing expenditure of $3,114,500 to establish a centralized electronic laboratory in Rome, became so bogged down in partisan strife that Armed Services Committee Chairman Carl Vinson of Georgia set it aside from the bill. He would not delay the whole measure "because of a dog fight between New Jersey and New York," he said.

Meanwhile, the Pentagon had enlisted support in the White House for its electronics centralization program. And it continued its pressure, starting in 1948, for hundreds of additional housing units in the Rome area to house incoming RADC people. Several Rome builders, including Rome-booster Al Pearsall, completed projects with no tenants yet in sight. Pearsall's Mohawk Gardens development went bankrupt because of the delay of RADC.

Pearsall and this writer, in 1950 vice-president of the Rome Chamber of Commerce, testified before Senate and House committees on behalf of Rome and secured inspection of the Rome base by influential legislators.

A few days before Congress adjourned, a separate bill, S-3727, was approved, giving the Secretary of the Air Force power to "establish or develop an Air Force Electronics Development Center at Grifiss Air Base, Rome, New York."

Since that time, when efforts have been made in the Pentagon to move RADC, the Air Force has been reminded that it is here by Act of Congress.

In the 1970's, when a serious effort was made by the Air Force to move vital parts of RADC, perhaps eventually all of it, this decision was thwarted by application of congressional pressures not yet understood by those uninformed of that struggle.

Grandpa always chuckled about the farmer who was plowing with a bull while a tractor was idle in the yard. A passerby asked why not use the machine?

The farmer replied: "I'm teaching this bull there's more to life than romance."

THE RFA STADIUM

In 1950 there was a growing need for a suitable place for RFA football home games. The team had never had a permanent field, playing at Oneida County Fairgrounds on upper Floyd Avenue, at the Rome Colonels' baseball park, for 60 years at any place big enough for a gridiron.

After the Rome Free Academy building was erected on Turin Street, the school board invested $30,000 for athletic facilities adjacent to the school. None of this fund provided for seating.

As early as 1944, Jim Kennedy, then vice-president of Rome Manufacturing Division of Revere, later company president, sent one of his staff, Louis Van Slyke, on a stadium inspection trip to Ohio, hotbed of high school football. He returned talking about a $300,000 stadium, causing his most avid followers to openly wonder "where will we get the money?"

Van Slyke, an optimistic extrovert, never gave up. Neither did Kennedy. They devised a catchy slogan, "Rome at Home in 50," and Kennedy directed Van Slyke to keep looking for something under $100,000 with 2,000-3,000 seats. Finally Van Slyke reported a smaller version of steel and concrete stands could be seen at Niagara University.

He gathered a committee of John Grant, popular RFA football coach; the Rev. David N. Boswell of Frist Baptist Church, a football star at Bucknell; Fran Regan, *Sentinel* sports editor; former Mayor John C. Schanz; Al Johnson, to handle the money; and Dave Townsend, always a sports booster. These men of enthusiasm began a person-to-person campaign for money.

Meanwhile, Van Slyke learned that a 4,000-seat structure might be available for around $60,000. But try as hard as it could, the committee faced failure, with a $20,000 deficit early in 1950. The idea appeared doomed.

Then Brad Barnard, publisher of the *Sentinel* and captain-quarterback of the undefeated 1913 RFA team, had an idea that worked.

Called into his office with Stan DeHimer, *Sentinel* advertising director and ex-star athlete, Brad told us: "We are going to do it. Sell 4,000 tickets at $5 each for the opening game. And you are going to help."

That game was only three and a half months away! There was no stadium, not even plans for one!

Barnard enlisted assistance of the Chamber of Commerce and the service clubs for a tickets-for-seats-yet-to-be-built drive. Construction contracts were let before the last $20,000 was raised. The game with arch-rival Utica Free Academy, originally scheduled to end the season, was moved up to be the first—in the still non-existant RFA Stadium.

Cannon Stadium and Seating Company, Niagara Falls, had the general $63,000 contract. All the work was done by Romans, Goerge Donahue the excavating, Cataldo Brothers and Sons the concrete work, Rome Iron Mills the steel.

And Van Slyke's boast was true: "Most of the money came from the small fry."

There were predictable problems, but finally the stadium was completed, a few days before the game date. An electronic scoreboard was installed by the *Sentinel* and, on September 22, 1950, RFA defeated UFA, 47 to 0, in the 60th anniversary game between the two—before 4,000 in $5 seats in the new stadium and 3,000 more in bleachers rented from Oneida, Boonville, Holland Patent, Prospect and Barneveld.

Van Slyke was in his glory. His boss gave him time off and he went up and down the streets selling several hundred tickets. Never before or since has Rome had a go-getter as the late Louie Van Slyke.

On the final day of the ticket drive, Brad Barnard personally bought the several hundred tickets yet unsold, sending us to Griffiss AFB with 300 or more for the troops and carrying dozens of others around with him, handing them out to *Sentinel* people and others like they were circus passes.

It took big men and women to make such a quick campaign come true. It was proven that Rome had them in 1950!

★   ★   ★

ROME'S MISSILE CRISIS

President Kennedy told the American people October 22, 1962 that the Soviets had installed nuclear missiles in Cuba. He had known it since October 16 of that year, the Pentagon having secured solid evidence late on October 15, now observed as the beginning of the Cuban Missile Crisis.

Senator Kenneth B. Keating of New York had been warning of the Soviet presence in Cuba since August 28, 1962. The White House paid little public attention.

We were in Washington a few days before the crisis became known. The administration, including President Kennedy, who addressed newspaper editors between October 16 and 22, had been stressing that the next Cold War confrontation might come over Berlin. Following the President's address to the editors, including this one, none asked Kennedy about Cuba! (After the crisis was over, we actually had a dream that we had risen to our feet and asked, "Mr. President, what about Cuba?" and was thereupon ushered from the State Department auditorium.)

That night, a colleague was told by former military classmates, "There is more to it than is being said." All the editors went home uninformed as to the truth, at least all we knew.

Between the time the President warned the nation and the day he was first made aware of the Soviet missiles, Rome air raid sirens sounded—accidentally. Few, if any, of the citizens responded as directed in warning placards distributed by Civil Defense.

Even more illustrative of the state of mind of Americans; on the night before the day when the U.S. was to stop a Russian ship, bringing on a possible nuclear conflict, the local siren sounded again. The people ignored it.

What do the phrases, "clean as a hound's tooth," "the lunatic fringe," "pussyfooting," "Mollycoddle," and "rubber stamp Congress," have in common? They were all coined by Teddy Roosevelt.

OUR LADY AND THE PRESIDENT

It was five months after the assassination of President Kennedy. President Johnson had ended a moratorium on social events at the White House. The American Society of Newspaper Editors was one of the first groups invited—some 400 of them, including wives —to meet with the new President at his new home.

So the editors gathered in the Rose Garden and waited. Mr. Johnson was settling a railroad strike in the Oval Office. The wives began reporting that their high heels were sinking into the sod. We gave Our Lady our checkbook to stand upon.

The crowd waited about 20 minutes. Then Mr. Johnson came out on the West Wing porch, off his office, and gave a Billy Graham sermon—a 15 minute exhortation about the goodness of America and the necessity to draw its people together. By the end of his fiery, passionate speech even the checkbook was sinking into the ground.

Then he invited the editors and their guests inside the White House, in jest asking each to pick up a candle from Lady Bird on the way in, these being days when the press was picking on the new President because, in his enthusiasm for economy, he was going around turning off White House lights.

Of course there were no candles. But there were five bars and two huge buffet tables, each with Texas steamship rounds at both ends. The White House apparently had no jiggers and the liquor, of all types, was poured from half-gallon bottles.

The Marine Band was split into its dance, symphonic, jazz and chorus groups in various main floor rooms. The President danced with many of the women, young military aides asking the wives to dance and then steering them into the arms of Lyndon B. Johnson, who towered above all of them. He must have whirled around with more than 60 flabbergasted but delighted females the hour or so he was on the dance floor.

The party lasted for two and a half hours—a real Southwestern bash. To our horror, we noted that some of the decorative fringe balls were missing from the massive drapes in the East Room, probably confiscated for souvenirs.

Twice more during his presidency we were in Mr. Johnson's

House—he always called it "your house." But it was never the same as that first time.

We cherish the line in Casey Jones' *Syracuse Herald* column the day following that 1964 country style wing-ding in the White House. The editor of the Syracuse paper wrote: "The last I saw of Johnson he was dancing with the wife of the Rome editor and they both looked as if they were having a good time."

Brick Hasfield says to avoid that run down feeling, wait for the green light.

MEET A SNOW SNAKE

In 1972, it was reported, on the *Sentinel's* editorial page, that a "snow snake" had been found under a log in Wright Settlement. The news came from Dave Wright, who had his tongue in his cheek. Dr. John Gabler subsequently identified the snow snake as a rare *Coluber Arcticus*, accompanying his opinion with a picture of one coiled on a tree limb.

The fame of that snake spread across the nation, Susan Myrick filing this report in the April 27, 1972 edition of the *Macon* (Ga.) *Telegraph*:

"Did you ever see a *Coluber Arcticus*? Snow snake, that is. I didn't either. But there are those who declare they have seen snow snakes."

"In the Rome (N.Y.) *Sentinel* letters to the editor have been pro and con on the subject of snow snakes, some persons declaring the snow snake puts its tail it its mouth and tolls along like a hoop. Southern children have heard about hoop snakes that make themselves into hoops by putting their tails into their mouths, but the hoop snake is not white as snow and the snow snake is believed to be pure white."

"A recent issue of the *Sentinel* carried a picture of what looked like a white snake woven in and out of small branches on a larger branch. It also looked somewhat like a snake made of white rubber.

"The photograph of the 'white snake' was made by a chap who signed himself, 'J. Gabler, Proprietor, Fort Rickey Game Farm.' Mr. Gabler wrote that he personally photographed the legendary snow snake, *Coluber Arcticus*, during a rare migration south of its arctic habitat.'

"Amused with the idea of a snow snake, and wondering if such a snake really exists, I began my search for evidence. The city library provided scanty information on snakes, but there were references to various snakes of the 'Coluber' family—blue racer (that Southern children call a black runner) is of that *Coluber* family, so is the coach whip. But the available books had no mention of a snow snake.

"I telephoned John McKay at the Museum of Arts and Sciences; he is a herpitologist and a wildlife man at the museum, and he never ever heard of a snow snake. There might be such a thing, he agreed, but he was doubtful. He referred me to Dr. T.P. Haines, professor of biology at Mercer University, who is a herpitologist. Dr. Haines said he 'doubts very much that there is such a thing as a *Coluber Arcticus*.' He added he could scarcely imagine a snake that could live at the Arctic Circle.

"Mr. McKay also suggested I telephone Dr. William Brode, Wesleyan professor of biology. Dr. Brode was vastly amused at the idea of a 'snow snake' and he, too, doubted its existence. He agreed with Mr. McKay and Dr. Haines that if it be a 'rare snake' it is rare, indeed.

"So, I shall not spend my winter days looking for a snow snake. I, along with the experts, doubt its existence." (End of *Macon Telegraph* column.)

We asked, in print: Not believe in snow snakes? That's like not believing in Santa Claus, that Columbus was the first to discover America or that Harry Truman couldn't have defeated General Eisenhower.

We commended Susan Myrick's efforts to spread the word about snow snakes and declared we had no desire to contend in intelligence with her learned advisors. We expressed the wish that if those who doubted our word, and that of the noted herpitologist,

J. Gabler, that they could consult Iroquois Indians, any of them being truly experts on snow snakes, particularly those stiffened into long shafts and used in a famous Indian winter game.

Some years ago our daughter-in-law said that just before Christmas she was visited by a jolly bearded fellow with a big bag over his shoulder. It wasn't Santa Claus. It was one of our grandsons, home from college with a semester's worth of dirty laundry.

It was 44° above zero, the first time in 25 days that the temperature in Rome had been above freezing. The countryside was covered with heavy wet snow and sleet, the mixture punctuated by gusts of heavy winds. Crazy weather, the paper said.

Overnight 11 persons had escaped unharmed from a fire at the Top Hat Restaurant, 111 Erie Blvd. West, and seven were homeless after a fire at 209 North George Street, corner of West Park.

The Oneida County Board of Supervisors was deadlocked 25 to 25, over election of a chairman. Republican Gilbert D. Pierce of Bridgewater finally won.

Some congressmen were agitating for a raise in pay, from $22,500 to $32,500.

Hinman's Apple Store, 220 South James Street, was selling apples for $1.75 a bushel and 50 pounds of potatoes for $1.25. Pot roasts were 33 cents a pound, hamburg two pounds for 89 cents at the Mohican Store.

And William A. Valentine took the oath of office as mayor of Rome. It was the beginning of 1964; he would serve 16 years.

Brick Hasfield says girls admired for their brains get kissed on their foreheads.

STEAK—INDIAN STYLE

Lorimer Rich, of Camden, was a gracious man of notable achievements (designer of the Tomb of the Unknown Soldier at Arlington, and of Rome's unique Tomb of the Unknowns overlooking Fort Stanwix), but, to us, one of his greatest was his knack of cooking a steak Indian style.

Friends would gather at Lorimer's and Martha's summer place at Osceola for wonderful hours of refreshment and conversation, the latter charitable as to others' character but magnificent, as hours went by, in broadening one's knowlege of the foibles of mankind.

Finally, time came for the host's backyard magic. There he would build a goodly sized bonfire of hard wood capable of sustaining live coals, all the while reminding his guests that a good fire took time and required patience, cooperation and liquid sustinence.

When the fire was down to a hot bed, Lorimer would coat a two-inch thick slab of prime round steak, five or six pounds, with salt and then wrap it in brown butcher's paper, enclosing the package in wet newsprint, several pages thick.

He would ignore all skeptics who insisted they were lucky that Ben Huntington was grilling a similar steak, without salt, the conventional way in the kitchen range.

Most fascinating was Lorimer's judgment as to time in the coals. He had an hourglass which he declared never failed; a tall glass filled with Jack Daniels and soda, slowly to be sipped, an empty condition declaring "the steak's done!"

A grand man, Lorimer Rich, of international distinction but never more in his glory than with friends and an Indian steak in his Tug Hill backyard.

A girl called her mother and said, excitedly: "Harry and I are engaged."

"In what?" her mother asked.

A ROOF WITH A VIEW

The old Rome Trust Company building, on the southeast corner of James and Dominick Streets, was a pile of rubble in late 1974. At that time it had been the Rome Trust office of Oneida National Bank, demolished in the Urban Renewal program to make way for Fort Stanwix National Monument.

Thousands may remember it for personal events—their first savings account, first mortgage or loan payment, the depository of their valuables, and the valuable financial advice dispensed there. It was where we kept renewing a $50 note in our young days when we were making less than that a week.

And it was the grandstand from which we witnessed, on news assignments, some of the now forgotten events of old Rome.

From the roof of that bank we saw Charles Lindbergh fly over Rome and from that vantage point we watched eclipses of the sun, passages overhead of dirigibles, both foreign and domestic, a big fire next door, and even a movie automobile "accident" at the American Corner.

The *Sentinel*, in a late 1920's public relations effort sponsored a hometown motion picture, the script of which called for a collision of two automobiles. The director had two cars slowly come into harmless contact, then set off a big cloud of smoke which covered the corner and much of the large crowd. The camera stopped, two wrecked cars were substituted for the first ones and when the smoke lifted the camera recorded a graphic accident scene, the hero valiantly trying to extract the heroine from the wreckage.

The corner by the bank also was the scene of one of Rome's classic legends. Engraved in Rome history is the remark of the owner of a horse which dropped dead there years ago.

"That's strange," he said, "he never did that before."

Brick Hasfield says it takes more brains to make out one's income tax than it does to earn it.

FORT STANWIX "CRISNED"

Life in Fort Stanwix, during its construction by British and provincial forces in 1758, as preserved in the journal of Ensign Moses Dorr of Captain Parker's Company of Colonel Williams' Massachusetts militia regiment:

"AUGUST 27—This day a child was buried belonging to Jersey Regiment. Four wimen were the barrers. Such a sight I never seen. Work of the fort goes on very fast.

"AUGUST 31—This day two men belonging to the York Regiment were wipt for disartion one had three hundred lashes and the other eight hundred. Nothing extrodenary.

"SEPTEMBER 6th—A squaw brought her papoose to the Jersey minister to be Baptised and it was performed with all the Seremoneys as Usaly with that soledness that it was admired by all that see it and as her husband was gone with the Armey she desired the Minister to pray for him.

"SEPTEMBER 23rd—About three o'clock the whole town of Sodom pulled down and sot on fire. There was a numer womans hutes that made great disturvens.

"OCTOBER 6—This day a number of our sic men went down the river and at about 12 o'clock as the Endions were from the fort a half a mile a number of the enemy fired upon them and killed one of their chiefs and in about half an hour after the people brouth the Endion with his heald scelpt. (Vienderwnta, an Oneida warrior, and two others were attacked in the woods near the incompleted fort by French Indians.)

"OCTOBER 7—About four o'clock the Endion King was buried in a coffin in the South Bastion of the fort and at his burrin there was fired three minnit guns. After this was done called the bastion the Onida. He was buried with his gun and hatchet.

"OCTOBER 15—This day a man belonging to the York regiment was wipt a thousand lashes and after ward drummed out of the regiment. Nothing extrodenery this day.

"OCTOBER 18—This day the river very high and floated several tents by reason of which a woman lost her life.

"OCTOBER 19—This day a number of vattoas want down the river and at 12 o'clock the fort is crisned called Fort Stanwix (after the British brigadier general in charge of the construction.)"

AND ON MAY 22, 1976—Fort Stanwix National Monument was dedicated—at 12 noon.

They tell this story at Rome Hospital:

After showing a nervous father his new-born child, the nurse asked, "Would you like to see your wife?" "No," he emphatically declared, "we haven't spoken in two years."

A BASKET OF JUNK

The Lady of Our House came home from an auction with the news that "they sold an old Edison phonograph, the kind with the big horn, and a case of cylinder records for $40." "Great," we replied, "where is it?" "Oh, I know that's cheap but I don't have room for anything like that, so I didn't bid." It would be worth a lot more today.

At the same auction, she was standing close by with no intention of buying anything and suddenly had to brush an insect from her ear. The auctioneer shouted: "Sold! to the lady over there," and Our Lady found she had purchased an antique ink well she now cherishes.

We are not auction prone, but when we were a young boy one of those sales started the hobby that has brought us much pleasure—an interest in Civil War history. Our father came home from a vendue with a box and a bushel basket filled with various items, mostly junk. Experts on auctions know how the auctioneer, when bidding lags, will keep adding to the goods being offered, "throwing in" this and that until he creates interest.

This had happened to Dad. They put up a box of junk and then added a basket filled with several things, including an old tool our father thought might be useful. So he bid a quarter for the lot and it was "knocked down" to him.

Among the miscellaneous articles he had bought was a large

book, "Frank Leslie's Illustrated History of the Civil War," a collection of wood cuts of camp and battle scenes. We pawed over that book from the time we were ten, wearing it to tatters, all the while creating an interest that has never subsided. We still have it, the binding and many of the pages torn almost to the point of uselessness. It rests in our attic and is not for sale!

Brick Hasfield says a senior citizen is one who can tell what used to stand where the parking lot is now.

NOT SO LONG AGO

This is a young country. For instance . . .

Our Mother, then a young, unmarried school teacher, saw President McKinley shot at the Pan-American Exposition, in Buffalo, September 5, 1901.

Her father (our grandfather of Potato Hill) saw President Abraham Lincoln (1809-1865) review Union troops at Fredericksburg, Virginia, in 1863.

Our paternal grandfather had a father who fought in the Mexican War.

We saw 1,864 veterans (North and South) of the Civil War at the 75th anniversary of the Battle of Gettysburg, July 1-5, 1938. Even more significant, we took a Confederate and a Union soldier to the very spot where the Southerner was attacking the Northerner, 75 years before on the very day (Pickett's Charge).

And we have great-grandchildren who should be living, according to averages, into the 2070's.

Brick Hasfield says a man can be known by the company he thinks nobody knows he's keeping.

WARNING FOR HUSBANDS

We are accused, particularly by The Lady of Our House, of being too personal in this space. Nevertheless, we must relate the tale of our Archie Bunker chair—if only for the protection of other male householders.

We spend countless profitable hours in a side-swing, rocker type of body receptacle in which we collect—and then often misplace—some of our best thoughts.

It all started when that chair suffered a defect of age. The device upon which it pivoted broke.

When the expert in such things came with his truck, Our Lady suggested, more than hopefully, we now recall, that the opportunity had arisen to have the entire chair renewed. Without collecting our views on the subject, she told the man we would follow the truck to his place for the selection of materials. We sort of liked the idea—a chair that worked, in new colors.

When the chair came back—properly balanced for operation in four directions and resplendent in its new coat—Our Lady hardly let us test it for fit when she declared its new covering did not match the carpet!

Like some politicians, we do not recall, but are now reminded when the subject comes up, that we said something about it probably being appropriate to renew the floor covering. We were comfortable in familiar surroundings, but after many years perhaps a woman should change things in her house—a little.

Anyway, for the next two weeks big swatches of available carpeting were strewn about the living room, dining room, stairway and upstairs hall. After much deliberation, involving advice from daughters and close friends, a choice was made—for future delivery.

When we sought to ascertain when the new carpet was coming, having satisfied ourselves that we could handle such a situation with a small checkbook surplus, we were turned aside with innocent remarks, like "I'm thinking about it" and "I can't make up my mind."

What was so difficult in deciding when the carpet man could send his expert putters-down? We did not sense the future.

Then, one evening when we were enjoying our new chair and watching Barney Miller, the voice we share the house with said something about papering the upper portion of the dining room walls, wondering aloud about style and size of chair rail and what color would accentuate the new living room.

We realized then what was ahead and with but a feeble joke about being manipulated to a good purpose, we said we knew just the painter she needed. Now it was the whole interior!

After Ray Wescott fashioned the chair rail and Mike Money did a fine job as a one-armed paperhanger (he had a pinched nerve which he ignored), we succeeded in capturing some of the crowded hours of Ron Staple, expert in matters involving brushes and colors. When we returned from the family's annual Canadian convocation we noticed that Our Lady was not pushing the project; something was bothering her, something she had to face.

When the painting was completed, we asked when the carpet would arrive. She said, again softly, that the carpet was at the store—we knew that, having paid half the bill months before—and would be quickly delivered once the floors had been redone. Floors?

Ignoring our bewilderment, she arranged with John Haley, senior and junior, to sand the old finish and apply a new one. That may sound simple but ask any man who has gone through living for several days in the kitchen, hopping from one spot to another to reach the bathroom.

Finally, the floors, up and down, were done, the carpet was delivered by Francis X. Donovan and skillfully placed by Dominick Gerace and his young helper. The house looked just fine. We were glad to have helped make someone we love happy— proud that we had thought of all those needed improvements!

Then, one night as we were watching Archie Bunker from his chair, the voice we live with began to wonder what kind and color drapes she would get. Drapes? What was wrong with those magnificent ones that drew so easily across the windows, a good arrangement we had had for more than a decade?

Age, she said. We muttered about drapes being the end of the rehabilitation program. No response.

Several days later, in a good mood, we were commending Our

Lady on her choice of colors and materials, confessing that while she certainly deserved a change we never thought we would be so anxious to meet her wishes and now were pleased that, with our customary thoughtfulness, her decorating problems were over, she said:

"I will be happy when I have that davenport recovered so that it matches the room!"

Davenport? Our sacred napping shelter? It hasn't been in the house long enough to get the fuzz off. It's practically new, no more than 10 years old. And not a sign of wear! And what will we do in late afternoon while our nest is undergoing such unnecessary treatment?

If there were any answers to these and other questions that kept stirring the issue, they have not pierced the mystery. That beautiful davenport, next to our chair our most precious instrument of ease, simply did not match the carpet, she declared, did not go with the drapes-to-be, did not mingle nicely with the walls, let alone the chair, and simply had to be readorned.

It was incomprehensible! We had a new interior because our favorite chair developed a list to starboard. We have long since realized that marriage is not so bad when a man has become accustomed to what his wife likes. We must admit the house looks fine and she certainly deserves the best. We are, in a way, proud of the way she spared us all of the project at one time. But it is absolutely necessary, even our duty to our peers, to warn other husbands: If your chair breaks, get a new one that matches your present furnishings! Quick!

★ ★ ★

TWO-SIDED EDITOR

State lotteries attract wide attention every time there are multi-million dollar winners. The lucky ones are few, the chance of winning first prize in New York being something like 1 in 12,271,512. There are no published figures on the dreams that fail to come true.

Lotteries go back for centuries, even before Nero, who would give his guests tickets for prizes such as a new abode or a slave. The Continental Congress provided for a lottery in 1776 to finance the American Revolution. Some of our first statesmen, led by Thomas Jefferson, supported such legalized gambling. By 1820, Congress had passed 70 lottery acts to raise funds for schools, roads and other public facilities.

The 1890 *Encyclopedia Britannica* declared the laws of every state in the Union were against "these schemes (but) they exist, a scourge to the poor, and a temptation to the weak."

All of which sounds familiar. When the New York State Lottery became law, we wrote an editorial for the *Sentinel* deploring the "public sanction of such temptation of people who could not afford the loss of precious money."

Within a few weeks, the Associated Press carried an item that we had won $300 in the lottery! We had to confess in print there was a difference between our public and our private opinions.

★ ★ ★

Brick Hasfield says some Americans spend $90 for jogging shoes and $900 for a riding lawnmower.

★ ★ ★

ERIE CANAL VILLAGE

Two kinds of folks visit Erie Canal Village, Rome's outstanding historical attraction. Those who have vivid memories of when homes were heated by wood and coal stoves and those who missed all those good and bad times.

The Village has a splendid collection of free-standing stoves, many of them from the Clarence Harden Collection. Mr. Harden contributed greatly to the success of the Village by donating his artifacts to the City of Rome. There would be no exhibit of old time vehicles, one of the outstanding attractions, without Mr. Harden.

We walk with memories when we take visitors to Erie Canal Village.

It always was fun to take grandchildren, when they were small, to the west side of Rome to see where the Erie Canal was started. It is an educational place.

The one-room school house is much like the one which introduced us to formal education. As a first-grader (there was no kindergarten), we sat in the third row (the first two were reserved for the grades called up to recite) and walked a couple of miles, each way, to get to school, no matter the weather. We remember once being punished for some misattention by being kept after school and made to fill the ink wells.

Later, in another county, we attended a two-room school, elementary grades in one, first two years of high school in the other. Then on to a boarding (preparatory) school and to college for a year, formal education ending, as we have explained, "when the family ran out of money, we ran out of educational attainments and the college ran us out." (We have since been asked to return to college and lecture on what it takes to succeed in newspaper work.)

The other takes-one-back-in-time place at the Village is the railroad depot, one of the last survivors of those small, weatherbeaten buildings that patiently wait by the tracks across the nation for the ravages of time.

The Rome and Fort Bull locomotive's whistle can be heard across the community on a quiet day. But the Village train does not make the haunting song of steel rails as it draws near nor the rattle of metal against metal as did the old-time trains when they drew into the station.

The young folks, still in their teens, believed us when we said we had hitched a horse or a team of horses to most of the type of vehicles shown in the Harden Museum and that the Canal Museum showed life the way it was on the great waterway. They were not quite prepared to take our word that we had started formal education in a one-room rural school, comparable to the Village's aged exhibit.

They had seen railroad depots and blacksmith shops, but never a horse being harnessed. The stable, with its big draft horses, was an outstanding attraction for them.

It should not be surprising in these days of motor cars, with horses a luxury, that a great majority of the people do not know how to put a harness on a horse. For most folks a blinker is a flashing light, a trace is something you put on paper and a collar goes around your neck. As for hame tug, breeching, crupper and belly band—what are those?

We should have been prepared. When these same grandchildren were six or seven years old, we took them to Upper Canada Village, which provides rides on wagons drawn by oxen and horses. "What's that in the road?" one asked. That grandchild had never seen horse droppings.

A lady called about the column we were writing, declaring: "I enjoy it as much as my husband."

There are proposals that "harmless" ill-doers, out on probation, be equipped with high-tech devices which will monitor their whereabouts at all times. This reminds us of the responder equipment strapped to roaming bull moose and their mates so that their location and state of life can be recorded.

Such technology was lacking in older days but the idea was the same in the establishment of "Jail Limits" from which probationers were not supposed to stray. Except, of course, to go to church and then only on Sundays when saloons ar d other tempting places were supposed to be closed.

A "Jail Limit" marker stands to this day in the yard of the Jervis Mansion, now part of the Jervis Library. All the others, as far as we know, no longer exist to mark out a territory in which those in trouble might roam, free of confinement in a jail cell.

Brick Hasfield says a girl with curves is often surrounded by men with angles.

AN ATTACK OF NOSTALGIA

It was Labor Day and in keeping with the occasion the Lady of Our House decided it was time to clean out the garage. That meant moving a lot of stuff into the driveway, scrubbing down the floor and carrying most of the same stuff, useful and useless, back into the garage where it would be more attractively displayed.

(It should be understood that the "garage" actually is a storage shed. It has not housed a car for some 60 years but is the repository for all those "wonderful old things about which something will be done sometime . . .")

It did no good to protest, so we cooperated with deliberate speed, muttering loudly about throwing away things, an unsuccessful protest from the start.

Then Our Lady fell into her own trap. Lugging a large cardboard box out of hiding, she suggested another task for us would be to go through it for anything valuable.

What a find! A collection of priceless memorabilia of prep school and college days—dance cards, programs which prove we sang solos in school musicals, pictures that show we were on a college football squad, old yearbooks, report cards, tuition bills and, best of all, packages of old love letters.

That was the last of work for that day for us. We pulled up a lawn chair and relived days when the burdens of the world were light, when the future was uncertain but rosy and the present delightful and, when there were girls who liked to write warm letters. The sampling of romantic days of 65 years in the past was all the more entrancing because of the inherent mystery. Who were some of those young ladies with whom we carried on such engaging correspondence? Some we recall with fondness, others now walk in unknown from the past.

Every demand for cooperation and resumption of labor from the lady with the mop and the broom was easily repulsed. All we did was threaten to read to her one of the love letters she had written those many years ago.

No man can clean a garage when he has an acute attack of nostalgia.

★   ★   ★

Mill Street is not named for the factories once in the area called East Rome. It was so termed in the early days of Rome for the grist mill, called "the red mill," located at the lower end of what is now Mill Street, at the Mohawk River, before it was canalized.

Built and operated by Dominick, James and Jasper Lynch, early landowners, it was the only mill of its type in this area and had a large patronage, farmers from throughout the region bringing their grain for grinding, paying for that service with every tenth bushel of the product.

"The red mill" eventually became a wrench factory and finally burned to the ground.

Brick Hasfield says a red light is where you wait for the cars you passed to catch up.

OLD FASHIONED DOCTOR

Our Boston granddaughter, Bobbi, once worried her grandmother (The Lady of Our House) with a severe cold. We heard this conversation:

"Bobbi, I am going to put an onion poultice on your chest!"

"No way, Gram!"

"Bobbi, I am going to brew some bitterweed tea and you drink it."

"No way, Gram!"

"Bobbi, I am going to make you sip a whiskey sling and put you to bed."

"No way, Gram!"

The usual response for a young, stubborn youngster? Not in this case. Bobbi is Dr. Barbara Philipp Pisegna, a staff pediatrician at Lahey Clinic, Burlington, Massachusetts. She had no faith in folklore medicine, even if administered by her grandmother.

★ ★ ★

A DAY IN HISTORY

He's a middle-aged man now but once upon a time, when he was about 12, he had long-remembered encounters with two national leaders, within less than an hour.

With his parents, the boy was standing in a long and wide second-floor corridor at the Hotel Statler in Washington. The American Society of Newspaper Editors was in annual meeting, the pre-banquet cocktail party in full flow.

The boy's mother would not permit her son to attend so the three, mother, father and son, were standing outside waiting for the banquet to begin. President Truman was to speak.

There was no one else in the large hallway until General Eisenhower, accompanied by two civilians, entered from the far end, walking toward the banquet entrance. He may have sensed something in the eyes of the young boy for the General made a left turn, walked 25 feet or so over to him, nodded to the adults and shook the boy's hand, asking: "How are you, young man?" The reply is lost in family history. General Eisenhower turned and walked on.

Shortly after, the boy and his parents were served the first course at the banquet, the boy talking unendingly over his soup, showing little interest in food.

A prominent U.S. Senator, who had obviously been upholding his well-known reputation by remaining too long at the cocktail party, walked in, stopped and put his arm around the young boy, muttering something—and drooled unsteadily into the youngster's soup.

A day in the life of our son, Peter!

Ever wonder why women button their clothing on the right and men on the left?

The Fashion Institute of Technology says that when buttons became popular in the 13th century, women that were prosperous enough to afford the new garments were dressed mostly by right-handed maids, who found buttoning to be easier with their right hand.

Shirts buttoned right over left were potentially hazardous to the sword-wielding man of the Middle Ages because, in drawing his weapon, which was almost always on his left side, he might entangle his cuffs in his shirt placket.

Brick Hasfield says home is where you can say whatever you please, because no one listens to you.

A WEDDING TO REMEMBER

The day started out like any other of the hot summer. The air was quiet, the sun increased in intensity, the dew disappeared quickly.

The families of a son and a daughter were to arrive around noon. There was to be a wedding at 3. Their sister, June Updike Rickard, was to be married to George J. Olney, Jr., in Westernville.

We went out for the *New York Times*, stopped by the store for bread. When we put it in the freezer the day changed. The interior was cool, the light was off, the fan had stopped. We panicked.

We called Sears, explaining that a big box filled with frozen food was slowly spoiling, that people were coming for a wedding. Could anything be done? Yes, said the concerned woman on the phone.

We left the cellar and walked into the back yard to spread the bad news. It could not have been 10 minutes before the repair truck stopped in front of the house. Mr. McDaniels, the serviceman, said he would have to have light so he inserted the cord of his trouble lamp into the receptacle serving the freezer. No light!

The main box fuse that replaced the exhausted one put the freezer back in service and now is the most costly device of its kind in the house, nearly $15 for the call, money we were happy, under the circumstances, to spend.

We had two new fluorescent bulbs for the bathroom. They came taped together. After calling Sears to say "thanks" for prompt service in an emergency, we went to the bathroom to do the bulb change. While trying to remove the tape we caused one of the long, white glass tubes to explode, wounding a hand, creating a miniature sonic boom and littering the floor, rug and appliances with hundreds of tiny pieces of glass, like dust, where people might walk with bare feet. It was three hours until the wedding, seven miles away.

The Lady of Our House came, muttered about our ineptness, and carefully cleaned up with a damp rag. She said, "You had better put a dollar in the thank-you box." We did.

Soon it was past noon and Our Lady left to go, with a friend, to the home where the wedding cake awaited transportation to Woods Valley for the reception, organized and supervised by special friends as a personal favor to us.

The two families arrived hungry and in the more and more worrisome absence of Gram—she had been gone for more than an hour on a 30-minute trip—we found the potato salad and a freshly baked ham in the refrigerator, made iced tea, located the rolls and pointed to the ice chest where beer and soft drinks were cooling. Where was she?

We had been ready for more than an hour, being of the type that gets to the depot 60 minutes early. We began to fret, more and more. The kids laughed. They knew us. Then, as time went on, they too became anxious. After all the wedding was at 3.

Forty-five minutes before the procession—the church seven miles away—she appeared, wet with perspiration, looking like she should go to a hairdresser instead of a wedding. "Did they bake the cake?" we started to ask.

"Don't you say another word," she said, in that voice we have come to recognize as a signal to disappear.

We learned later that the three-tiered cake had begun to yield to the heat and had almost collapsed by sliding apart while in transit, to the point where the volunteer baker had to be summoned to make repairs.

Trying to save time, we drew her bath, turning on the water at a cool temperature. After she bathed and dressed, in the fastest time of our 55 years together, she came down looking lovely and asked,

"Why is the water so dirty?" In the midst of her small crisis, the water system had coughed up a big slug of dirt into the tub in which she was sitting.

We arrived just in time at the Westernville Presbyterian Church for a wedding filled with love, respect and acknowledgment of God's blessings. The bride and groom were escorted to the altar by their seven children, her three, his four. It was a joyous event that swept the audience to the point of approving applause at the first kiss.

The emotional face of the Lady beside us expressed it best; now both widowed daughters had found love and happiness again. In the applause, we did not know whether to laugh or cry with joy, so we did an impulsive bit of both.

The reception lasted four hours; no one seemed to mind the searing heat. Many of the guests attended in sports clothes, there was a horseshoe tournament, some young folks did gymnastics, a band played ear-shattering rock, disco and country music. The bride had changed her wedding dress for blouse and shorts and during the festivities she and her husband walked up the hill to the side of the ski slope where they had met and sat under a tree, holding hands, among what may have been clumps of poison ivy.

Many wore name tags. Ours read: "Father of the Bride."

A reader once asked us if Grandma ever served rabbit meat on Potato Hill and, if so, how.

She certainly did, raising them in pens alongside the chicken house. We never liked eating rabbit because we thought of them as pets, because they had a funny smell when fresh dressed, and because Grandpa once told us you had to be careful about worms in wild rabbits.

Grandma cooked them as she would chicken and on Potato Hill a young grandson ate what was put before him so we've eaten rabbit, with eyes closed most of the time, but not since then. Some folks consider rabbit the making of a gourmet meal. Not for us.

★   ★   ★

GLAUCOMYS VOLANS

When our son, Peter, and his family moved to Rome from Buffalo, they did not realize they were inheriting an acquaintanceship with *Glaucomys volans*. This flying squirrel, smaller than the grays, makes a delightful pet, we have been informed, if one does not mind its habit of sleeping all day and running around in the attic, making continuous sounds all night.

It really can't fly. It glides, with the aid of a loose membrane along each side, like a nimble parachutist. We've seen it in flight and can testify to its agility.

When our son sought assistance, we contributed our cage trap, mostly suitable for chipmunks and, sure enough, there was *Glaucomys volans*, confined and obviously worried about the future. In a hurry, our son let the flying squirrel out within a block of his house—and had the same squirrel, or its twin, in the trap the next morning.

He solved the problem by carting the trap outside the city several miles and releasing the flying squirrel near shelter. After catching three, the problem seemed solved until a new family settled in three or four years later.

His was our first experience with flying squirrels. We do have some knowledge of gray squirrels, particularly our weather forecasting gray which some folks call our rat with the educated tail. It is the tail that in the fall conveys knowledge of the weather ahead: Straight up, normal times; straight back, an easy winter; tucked about the ears, bad times ahead. The record is as good as that of some adult observers.

Gray squirrels are not well liked by utility companies, farmers and gardeners who rate them low on the list of friends. We reject them when they come up with ways to raid our bird feeders, although in recent years we have won that contest with a novel barrier on the poles that they do not pass.

Foresters held gray squirrels in high esteem, knowing that these four-footed Johnny Appleseeds play an important role in reseeding woodlands, burying more nuts than they can possibly eat.

We think of squirrels as playful backyard inhabitants, not realizing that in 1842 more than 450,000 grays marched across

Wisconsin, devouring everything they liked. We do not know who took that census, but that's what it says.

And only a few years ago, tens of thousands of these members of the *Sciuridae* family roamed the mountains of western North Carolina in search of food, a killing early frost having disturbed their life cycle.

Brick Hasfield says drive-in banks make it possible for cars to meet their real owners.

"SLIPS IN TYPE"

Newspaper folks like to josh colleagues by collecting their "slips in type," such as:

"The New Miss America will be drowned before a nationwide audience."—The Associated Press.

"Mr. Smith, who has been very ill for the past week, is still under the car of Dr. Jones."—Hudson, N.Y. *Sentinel*.

"The firemen carried the horse to the top of the ladder."—Hopewell, Va. *News*.

"The bus crunched through the front door of a tavern, injuring four men heated at the bar."—New Brunswick, N.J. *News*.

One of the best, from the Rome *Sentinel*, was not a typo. An ad for Elmer Preston's Music House (years ago a next door neighbor on North James Street) told this romantic story:

"You will want these records in your collection—Love Me—Hold Me Tight—I Couldn't Sleep a Wink Last Night—Oh, What a Beautiful Morning—People Will Say We're in Love."

We once wrote, in a *Sentinel* editorial, "If Lincoln were alive today, he'd roll over in his grave," neglecting to say that it was a quote from Gerald Ford, who borrowed it from someone else.

PROFESSOR VS. EDITOR

When our son was in Bucknell University he had a choice of taking his Mother to a concert or staying in his room finishing a paper on the influence of aviation on North and South American relations. He had to have a good mark to survive.

We volunteered to look over his work while he took his Mother to hear the music. He warned that his professor insisted on well-developed, long paragraphs. We told him to go along, certainly a newspaper editor knew more about long paragraphs than some college professor.

Later our son wrote home: "Tell Dad I passed, but the paper came back marked 'C plus—it would have been a B plus if the paragraphs had not been so short.'"

After that he insisted on getting through college on his own.

Brick Hasfield says a tourist is one who wants to be where there are no tourists.

For years Maurice G. Steele was our philosopher in residence. Here is an example of his contributions to an often struggling columnist.

"Evidence of the alarming rate at which we are using existing energy is readily available if one listens to sounds. He will hear automobiles, trucks, motorcycles, diesel-powered locomotives, lawn mowers, snow blowers, electric saws, airplanes and radios and television sets. And these are not all of the energy consumers.

"Contrast this with an observation made at the turn of the century. Then we might hear someone shoveling snow, pushing a lawn mower, chopping wood, the neighing of horses, the lowing of cattle, the clucking of chickens, the tinkling of a piano. Only the far-off whistle of a distant locomotive would suggest the coming advent of vast energy expenditures which even then were threatening.

CHRISTMAS TREES BY UPS

No longer is there an argument at our place over a suitable Christmas tree. The Lady of Our House would decide the appropriate time to get a tree was the afternoon of an important football game, no matter what the weather. And it was not proper to cut the first good-looking, well-shaped tree; it was necessary to look the entire lot over before such a momentous decision.

It took us four decades to realize that Christmas tree cutting did not have to be an annual family disruption. We finally learned to shut up and follow her from tree to tree, saw in hand. When she pointed to The Tree, we simply flopped down and sawed, our contribution insignificant.

That has now changed. Seven years or so ago, the two of us helped our grandchildren in Boone, North Carolina, Tom and Kay Philipp, plant several hundred Christmas trees on the steep hillside in front of their mountain home. Now they supply us with a Christmas tree every year—a five-foot Frasier Fir arriving in a large cardboard cylinder from North Carolina, via UPS.

Trees we helped plant on a slope on which neither of us could hardly maintain our balance. Trees that exude loving remembrance through the season, never dropping a needle.

Brick Hasfield says flirtation is attention without intention.

PRECIOUS DAYS AND NIGHTS

The talk among 16 adults for two weeks at the five-cabin complex on Lake Mississagagon, Ontario, concentrated on persistent heat (94-96 six consecutive days), Momma and Poppa loons with a back-riding little one on the lake, and the six great-grandchildren with a supervised run of the place. Usual questions like "Did you catch anything?" and "What's to eat tonight?" were subdued in the heat wave.

It was the 31st straight year that we have gathered at that lovely lake. The place belongs to Bill and Babe Tibble but we feel like we own it, certain that some day those great-grandchildren, some barely two, will be bringing their brood to Mississagagon. The grandchildren of four and three years in our first year there (1957) are now mothers and fathers of the little ones that confuse us—"Which one is that?" and "Who do they belong to?"

This year was about the same as the others, except for the weather and the baby loon. Many will not care but there may be a few who will be interested in another annual report.

Our place as master of the fishing fleet has been relinquished to younger folks who had a fruitless first week (virtually no bites) but an exciting second with four-pound bass, walleye and pike. Our knowledge of acid rain increases yearly; 30 years ago Mississagagon produced strings of fish daily. Now the catches are far less frequent and the fish smaller.

The loons, sometimes close by and watchable from the docks, sometimes far across the lake and observed from boats, were a constant study in nature. The little one would ride on its mother's back while the father fished for small minnows for the youngster. Periodically, the mother would partly submerge to dunk the baby into the water for a class in aquatic skills and then sink down to permit the little one to climb back aboard.

With the baby in the water, both father and mother would stand straight up and spread their wings, insisting the baby try the same. It would a few times and then look around for its living platform. Each day it grew closer to the time of leaving to go alone on its own. We wondered if there was a mate growing up in some of the bays down the lake.

All of us watched for the loons when we arose; we could hear but not interpret their plaintive calls during the night. Once, after midnight, there was a sharp sounding of loon alarm and our adults arose fearful something had happened to the young one. Early an expedition embarked on a search, returning to report that the loons were safe in the bay around the point. Our Lady happily went about enjoying herself with her young ones and with her unexpected mission—the little sweater she was making for an expected great-grandchild has to be matched. The diagnosis is twins!

A red fox walked across the road to the compound one morning and early walkers reported raising large coveys of grouse.

The money exchange was 16 to 19 cents, in our favor, fluctuating in response to unsteady financial status in the states. Last year one American dollar produced $1.29 Canadian.

The exchange rate is not the whole story. Gasoline was around $2.25 an American gallon. A 24-can case of Canadian beer was $23.35, less deposit of 10 cents a can. A bottle of liquor? Forget it —double or more American prices. Yet it is a nice feeling to leave a Bank of Montreal branch in the village 14 miles away with considerably more than when you entered.

Evening group menus (we are on our own until supper) ran from steak from Boston, chicken 'n' biscuits, ham with fixin's, chicken divan, spaghetti, a Chinese meal, corned beef and cabbage, chicken in batter, pig hocks and sauerkraut (not well received by the majority) leftovers and a fish fry. And always beautiful desserts, contributed by our expert younger girls and Babe, the landlady.

We took a brief course in child psychology. The young great-grandchildren had a problem in identification of great and ordinary grandparents. The two-year-olds would be told to "take it to great-grandma" and they naturally, would go to their grandmother. Or, "great-grandpa has something for you," and they would go searching for their grandfather.

We sought to solve this mental confusion by suggesting they call the two elders "G-G." That soon turned into "Gee, Gee" which is fine with the founders of this fourth generation but still baffling to bubbling-over youngsters.

We always have fireworks—legal in Canada—and this year's display was the best year, the result of the formation of a "Light Up Their Sky" committee which raised more than $100 for the two-night display.

Both sides of the border seemed more open, the Canadian customs agent greeting us without questions, saying "go on, enjoy." On the return to the U.S., the polite American inquired only about nationality with a declarative statement, "You are an American citizen!"

As those who may read these reports know, the family gathering in Canada, two weeks of lazy days on the shore of an unmarred lake, is the highlight of our year. We are glad there are others coming along to fulfill the joys after we have said farewell to Mississagagon.

Annually there is published a camp newspaper, The Blab. This year it carried a poem, "Canadian Legacy," by Henriette Gibson (our daughter-in-law, Lyn) which sums up for all of us our feelings. . .

"Twas yesterday—or just as near/when first the clan appeared right here/and built a legacy. Of memories of sounds and sights/ of kids—now grown—of starry nights/of smells and meals, of loons and walks/of fish, so big, outhouses, talks. Of costume parties, birds and rain/and here we are, all once again. But now these kids, they bring their own/the legacy has grown and grown. The circle is closed/complete the legacy goes round."

Once, when we declared there would be no camp report in our column, a granddaughter left us a note:

"Once again, the night before I am to leave this special place, I lie in bed and sense deep sadness, crying silent tears. I can remember doing the same for 27 other years, since I was a young child. Yet today, when I asked Wise Grandfather if he would write all this in his column, he said: 'I don't know. Nothing happened to write about,' Not true, Wise Grandfather!

"What is it about this precious place that makes it so sad each year to leave? Security, wearing old, smelly clothes, no one caring. Laughing together, eating too much, and no one caring. Swimming and walking and fishing and bird watching. The deep heavens at night, the blue skies, the water washing the shore at night. No worries, no cares—a simple, easy, loving, secure life, deep in the heart of those who love.

"Great beauty all around, Canadian forests, lakes, blue skies, fresh air, clean waters. The picture is clear, even when I'm not here. A wonderful place to expose children to the wonders of their life, so much spiritual nourishment for all of us, as it was here while I, too, was growing up.

"Please, don't ever say there is nothing to write about, Wise Grandfather. I have lived every minute of two lovely weeks in a beautiful, precious place with my family and stored away treasured memories, wonderful possessions for my little girl.

"How lucky I am, how lucky all of us as we look forward to

next year's togetherness. Wise Grandfather, there is much to write about—and remember!"

Dr. Barbara Philipp-Pisegna says it better than we can.

★ ★ ★

Brick Hasfield says a psychiatrist is the last guy you talk to before you talk to yourself.

★ ★ ★

OUR EDITORIAL BOARD

For many years we have enjoyed lunch at the Rome Club with what we once called our "editorial board." We no longer require its weighty advice but we try to be present Monday through Friday.

It has consisted, and still does, of from 5 to 12 friendly males of various situations in life, all experts on past, present and future events, each confident they have the answers to all problems, great and small.

They discuss the troubles of the presidency, the American Revolution, the power of women, the futility of life under present circumstances, the sure fate of the world, the deficiencies of the Congress, the federal deficit, the movies, TV and current political foibles—any subject that may deliberately or inadvertently be brought to attention.

The unspoken purpose, of course, is to shed new light on inbred prejudices, historical misconceptions, political loyalties, false knowledge and useless disciplines.

These daily occasions have been huge successes except for a minor flaw, to wit: No matter how much new evidence is introduced, lack of knowledge corrected, new light shed on abstruse situations or relationships with fellowman improved, the previous opinion, prejudices and errors in thought return to each of us, unchanged and firmly entrenched, when the identical discourses arise days later.

So intense may such deliberations become that one noon a

regular attendant, who likes to talk and does, declared to the waitress, after a long dissertation upon some subject in which the others were uninterested:

"If I have had my lunch, please bring me my check. If not, please bring me the special."

★ ★ ★

IT'S IN THE BLOOD

The job of reporter is the best in the newspaper business. We wanted to be one from early in life when an aunt, a writer of children's stories, said the way to begin was to start. We were brought up on her fairy tales, in which the characters were light bulbs.

Our Mother raised us on the basic principle: "You can be what you want to be if you try hard enough." An English teacher in preparatory school insisted we write the same themes over and over, while encouraging us, with another, to found and publish a weekly school newspaper of doubtful merit. We always thought the title was good: "The Walking Leaf."

When we answered a classified ad and became a *Sentinel* reporter, our only qualifications were a desire to write and the ability to type—with all fingers. If we had not had a wife and child, we would gladly have been a reporter without pay.

That child, Shirley, inherited the same stirrings, becoming a newspaper reporter and publications editor on her way to a highly successful public relations career.

After graduation from Syracuse University School of Journalism, she worked one summer in the *Sentinel* newsroom as a vacation fill-in. We now jointly chuckle about this—when vacations were completed, we had no need for another steady reporter. How does a father tell a daughter she's through?

She solved that problem by coming into our office to say: "I will be leaving in a week. I have a reporter's position with the *Watertown Daily Times*."

"Does your father know about this?" we asked with a straight face and inner smile. "No," she said, "but I will tell him at dinner tonight."

And she did, with grace and dignity. The family does not see much in that episode; father and daughter do.

She was the one who discovered the 5-cabin complex on Lake Mississagagon, two years before the family began, 31 years ago, our annual joint vacations. We all salute her for this.

Shirley also led the combined family drive for years to have us "write a book," constantly offering to help with typing and reading proofs, never able to excite one who had no driving desire to go over the old stuff he had written for 18 years.

Only the Lady of Our House knows about this late date enterprise. We hope the secret is kept until we call a session with our children to "discuss something you all should know."

★ ★ ★

YOU CAN RETIRE!

We are fortunate that after 50 years and 15 days with the same newspaper we are privileged, now 11 years in retirement, to retain our old office and to be able to come and go as we please.

We were thinking the other day about retirement. You work, you raise a family, you start with little, aside from the love and support of a good woman, you do your best. There isn't a day that you are not happy at your work. You like your job and feel lucky to have it.

Then one day the children are grown and married, the mortgage is paid and you suddenly realize time has gone faster than you realized. You can retire!

All your life you have heard that retirement is a bore. Your wife says she didn't marry you for lunch. OK. Retirement may not be for everyone. But it is fun when you can still work, doing what you like, in your own way as always and in your own time.

All this personal thought leads to the reality that more folks are retiring—and earlier. Increased life expectancy means more years of retirement. The average life span from birth now is more than 69 for men, 76 for women. That's average. And men and women who reach 70 can expect to live well beyond the expectancy figure.

Why do women live longer than men? Some day we'll look into that. Or maybe we'll leave well enough alone.

ABOUT THIS BOOK

For more than 18 years we have written a weekly column in the Rome *Sentinel*, mainly for our own enjoyment, partly as a repository for personal reactions that did not fit the editorial page, for which we were responsible for more than 30 years. We have had no compelling desire to write a book, even though our family kept insisting. Then came a suggestion from George and Shirley Waters, friends and newspaper associates, which we could not ignore.

The Lady of Our House, our children and others in the family will welcome this effort. We've tried to keep it a secret. Margaret McCarthy, for more than four decades our "office wife," would have been pleased to relieve us of typing and proof reading, while assisting with the usual beneficial criticisms. We miss her.

Bertha Evans, who for years had put the output of our old-style manual typewriter into type, has helped greatly.

This collection of often unrelated pieces from the column has memories of our early life with maternal grandparents, days with our father and mother on their farm, and recollections of a 61-year career as a reporter, editor, columnist and executive with the *Sentinel*.

Brick Hasfield deserves a special word. He was an odd character, of indeterminate age, who today might be called "not all there." To us, in childhood, he was wise as to how to trap skunks, catch big fish, recognize wild animal tracks, safely handle a gun and enjoy the outdoors. Over the years we have sought to honor his memory with "sayings," some relating to his unique wisdom.

This book is dedicated to our wife, Dorothy, and to our children, Shirley U. Kudla, June U. Olney, Peter S. Updike, and to Maggie McCarthy. Our editorial "we" in this book often encompasses the Lady of Our House.

We should also acknowledge a non-relative who, over the years, has kept insisting: "You should write a book, hundreds of folks would go to the library to read it."

974.762 UPD
Updike, Fritz S.,
Fritz S. Updike's Potato
 Hill and other recollec
$13.95 03/27/97 ABT-2076

AUG. 1 3 1998

OCT. 0 2 2000

APR 2 7 2006

AUG 25 '08

PROSPECT FREE LIBRARY
915 Trenton Falls St.
Prospect, New York 13435
(315)896-2736

MEMBER
MID-YORK LIBRARY SYSTEM
Utica, N.Y. 13502

A0001500047681